ADVANCE PRAISE for Tom Cronin's WRITING AS A PERFORMING ART

"WRITING AS A PERFORMING ART is absolutely marvelous. I thought I'd try it out on our 17-year-old son and use it to teach him a few things...He devoured it." Vince Bzdek, Editor, Colorado Politics and Colorado Springs Gazette, and former Assistant Editor, Washington Post.

"WRITING AS A PERFORMING ART is much more than a style book. I have been a writer all my life and never have come across a better boot camp-- it's a helpmate and guiding angel. It cultivates the Inner Editor...." Duncan Newcomer, podcaster, author, theologian, Belfast, Maine.

"Incredibly valuable...everyone should read it and take it to heart." Rhonda Van Pelt, veteran reporter and editor, Pikes Peak Bulletin

PRAISE FOR CRONIN'S OTHER BOOKS

IMAGINING A GREAT REPUBLIC: POLITICAL NOVELS AND THE IDEA OF AMERICA: "This is a grand tour of American literature. Its underlying ideas, insights, and conceptual structures make the book especially valuable. I'm in admiration of how Cronin engages these texts deeply ..." Thomas Barden, <u>Steinbeck Review</u>

PARADOXES OF THE AMERICAN PRESIDENCY (Cronin and Genovese): "One of the most clarifying books on presidential leadership—a modern classic." Warren Bennis

LEADERSHIP MATTERS (Cronin and Genovese): "An absolute tour-de-force...." Doris Kearns Goodwin, prize winning historian.

THE STATE OF THE PRESIDENCY: "An exceptionally intelligent work that comes along just when we need it." <u>The New Yorker</u>

DIRECT DEMOCRACY: "Cronin has given us a beautiful book." Everett Carll Ladd

WRITING AS A PERFORMING ART

on taking it to the house ...

Thomas E. Cronin

Trenton, Georgia

Copyright © 2022 Thomas E. Cronin

Print ISBN: 978-1-64719-648-6
Ebook ISBN: 978-1-64719-649-3

All rights reserved. No part of this publication may be reproduced, stored in a retrieval system, or transmitted in any form or by any means, electronic, mechanical, recording or otherwise, without the prior written permission of the author.

Published by BookLocker.com, Inc., Trenton, Georgia.

Printed on acid-free paper.
Cover painting by author Tom Cronin

BookLocker.com, Inc.
2022

First Edition

Library of Congress Cataloguing in Publication Data
Cronin, Thomas E.
Writing As A Performing Art: on taking it to the house… by Thomas E. Cronin
Library of Congress Control Number: 2021951094

"The art of writing has for backbone some fierce attachment to an idea."
Virginia Woolf

"I have always felt that the first duty of a writer was to ascend — to make flights, carrying others along if he could manage it. To do this takes courage, even a certain conceit."
E.B. White

"There is nothing to writing. All you do is sit down at the typewriter, open a vein, and bleed."
Red Smith

"A writer is someone who has taught his mind to misbehave."
Oscar Wilde

"Writing a book is a horrible, exhausting struggle, like a long bout of some painful illness. One would never undertake such a thing if one were not driven on by some demon whom one can neither resist nor understand."
George Orwell

DISCLAIMER

The ideas, content, and opinions in this book are solely those of the author. This book is provided on an "as is" basis. The publisher accepts no responsibility for the author's views.

This book was written to encourage nonfiction writers to consider counsel that might improve their writing.

A careful reading of this work is likely to improve your writing and inspire you to write more bravely. However, reading this book, even two or three times, cannot guarantee writing improvement or publication of your work.

Good writing requires uncommon time commitments and experimentation.

Neither the author nor the publisher will be liable for any damages arising out of or in connection with the use of this book.

Readers of this book will profit from reading several of the books listed in the Recommended Reading section located at the end of the book. Consider, too, taking a writing course at your local college and joining a writer's workshop sponsored by a local independent bookstore.

- Book will best be preserved at room temperature
- Book can be read before, after or with meals
- Book has no expiration date yet is best read in the next few days
- Book should be kept away from children under the age of seven and suspected terrorists

- Book can be underlined, highlighted or marked up in any way
- Book should be passed on to other would-be writers
- Send suggestions, corrections and contrarian opinions to the author at tcronin@coloradocollege.edu

Thanks for your understanding. Enjoy.

Contents

Preface 1
Why Write? 5
"Don't Get it Right, Get it Written" 13
Selecting a Topic 23
Researching Your Topic 27
Developing and Testing Hypotheses 31
Beginning to Write 37
Outlining and Focus 39
Writing Honestly 43
Writing to Convince and Persuade 47
Revising 49
Selecting Words Carefully 55
50 Pet Peeve Words 59
Let's Hear it for Everyday Words 61
Let Verbs Do the Heavy Lifting 63
Use Qualifiers Sparingly 67
Avoid Doubleheaders 71
Spare Us "Twinkies" 77
Be Correct 79

On the Other Hand: Dueling with the Grammar
    Police 81
More Usage Suggestions 91
New Challenges 93
Additional Style Suggestions 97
Tables and Numbers 103
Quotations and Citations 105
Leads and Conclusions 109
Format and Presentation 113
Writer's Block 115
Writing as a Performing Art 119
Footnotes 129
Helpful Works on Style and Usage 137
Thanks 143
About the Author 145

Preface

"Writing as a Performing Art: on taking it to the house..." began as a modest pep-talk handout I wrote one fall weekend when I was a visiting professor of Politics at Princeton University.

Princeton is one of the most writing-intensive universities in the nation. I was advising dozens of juniors and seniors writing theses of considerable length and I wanted to motivate them as well as clarify my suggestions and expectations.

At the time, the whole town was plastered with signs exhorting "Fight Tigers, Fight!" and "Win Tigers, Win!" as the Princeton Tiger varsity football squad faced a tough Ivy League adversary on a Saturday afternoon.

Instead of going to the game, I sat down a few neighborhoods away and wrote "Write Tigers, Write!" It was intended to fire up my students about their writing projects — in the same spirit that the university alumni and public relations staffs were pumping up their partisans to go all-out in cheering on their football team.

Young writers, just like ballplayers, need fans, cheerleaders and coaches, and I gladly accepted that role and wanted my students to "take it to the house" (to borrow a colloquial football metaphor) just as much as the Tiger football fans were cheering on their team to achieve multiple big-play scoring breakthroughs. By "house," I mean audience.

My handout was a success and it morphed into an article, *The Write Stuff,* published by the American Political Science Association. Prentice-Hall publishers distributed a similar booklet for a couple of years to help promote "Government by The People," an American politics college text I co-authored.

Writing as a Performing Art builds on those earlier essays yet, more importantly, evolves from decades of teaching and writing and my ventures as a newspaper columnist and writer.

I love writing and love reading works on stylish and readable writing. Among the helpful are those by: E.B. White, William Zinsser, Rudolf Flesch, Theodore Bernstein, James Kilpatrick, Peter Elbow, John McPhee, Helen Sword, Steven Pinker, Stephen King, Anne Lamott, Anne Curzan, John R. Trimble, Mary Norris, Laura Brown, Trish Hall, Martin Amis,

Natalie Goldberg, George Orwell, John Nichols and Sylvan Barnet. Others are cited in the bibliography.

tcronin@coloradocollege.edu

Why Write?

One of my friends and co-authors, Bob Loevy, explains that he loves to write to call attention to new ideas or get readers to consider new facts. He recalls his reporter days when he covered a story at a large local hospital about a young boy awaiting an emergency operation who needed blood. Bob wrote the story for his city newspaper, emphasizing how much this youth needed blood. His story spread the word and within a day or two 300 people had lined up to volunteer the blood and the young man lived.

Writers write because they want to shine a light on injustice, expose hypocrisy and lies, educate, entertain or just draw attention to what they think is important.

Writing is a way of crystallizing ideas, reporting research results, outlining plans.

George Washington's war against the British benefitted from a young immigrant with an agitational mind and talent for pamphleteering. His name was Thomas Paine and he wrote "Common Sense" in early 1776. He explained why "these free and independent states" needed to fight England for their rights. "These are the times that try men's souls.

The summer soldier and the sunshine patriot will, in this crisis, shirk from the service of his country; but he that stands it now, deserves the love and thanks of man and woman."

And then Paine shared his rallying cry against tyranny and why Americans had to persevere. His written word went what we call today "viral," with more than a half-million copies circulating within months. It inspired, mobilized and became one of the most effective weapons in America's war of independence. Thomas Jefferson's Declaration of Independence was written five months later. Their writing mattered. (They "took it to the House" of Parliament and King George III.)

Writing is hard, and scary, and exhilarating. The fear of writing is normal, natural and never fully goes away. Even the most accomplished writers admit the hardest part is getting started. Cranking up is hard to do.

What explains the fear of writing? People worry that everything they might write has already been written, and probably said better. We fear making mistakes or inviting unwelcome criticism.

An Imposter Syndrome angst looms over every craft —the notion that someone will discover we are pretending to be someone who we are not or writing something we don't know enough about. Yet most things worth doing involve at least some imitating, pretending, copying and borrowing.

Beginning to write is a little like beginning to climb a mountain. It is scary yet can be fun. Yes, others have already done it faster and more gracefully. Yet, we can do it too. One step at a time. You are not an imposter, you are out on your own journey, exploring, playing and being present.

It takes courage for any of us to take a pen up and write in the shadow of Shakespeare and Steinbeck, compose in the shadow of Beethoven and Dylan, paint in the shadow of van Gogh and Picasso. But how unfortunate it would have been had Shakespeare concluded that playwrights before him had written everything worthy to be written and thus his views and writings weren't needed.

Initial writing exercises don't need to be demanding. Think of thank-you notes, love letters, book or movie reviews, texting, journals and diaries. People write for assignments, to share stories, to earn a living, to protest or just to explore what is out there.

Writers write to celebrate courage, character and prowess. That's what the storyteller Homer did. A people without storytellers would be confused about who they are, where they came from and what they might become.

That's why we profit so much from the Old and New Testaments, and from writers like Leo Tolstoy, Victor Hugo, John Steinbeck and Toni Morrison. They helped us remember our past and understand the human condition.

Another reason many writers write is to help us navigate through the complexities of life. We all endure pain, loneliness, fear and hope, and we all see both beauty and tragedy. Writers reveal our common human bonds. They let us know we are not alone, and they help us search for better possibilities, and for hope and truth. They write about what is important and what is good.

Another friend and occasional co-author, Michael Genovese, shares that we write as an obligation to ourselves as well as neighbors. "We believe we have something to say. ... Writing helps us think through and sort out the paradoxes of the human condition. In explaining the world to others, we also seek self-understanding." By writing we educate ourselves, he adds, and "clarify our views and come to grips with a messy world."

Another reason to write is to speak up and talk about values and ideas you care about. There are many cherished, yet competing, political and economic values such as liberty, equality, efficiency, justice, security, community and the rule of law. But reasonable people disagree about how much each of these should be maximized or how best they can be reconciled. Reasonable people have always disagreed about these matters, and always will. That's why we have political parties, elections, judicial systems and politics in general. And that's why countless writers write to share their points of view and try to persuade others of their views.

Plato wrote to justify the need for highly educated, virtuous, hierarchical leadership. Martin Luther King, Jr. wrote and spoke about the need for tolerance, justice and the need to live peacefully with one another. Shakespeare wrote to warn us about the arrogance of power and the temptations of greed, jealousy and flattery. Rachel Carson's "Silent Spring" shared her research about better farming practices and how to save lives — and her writing made a huge difference.

Many writers write because they are storytellers. One of my neighbors is a prize-winning author of young adult and children's books. Dian Curtis Regan says, "There is such joy in having an idea nudge you until you sit down and find the story that's wanting to be told," and then eventually see it in book form. "Writers strive to get to that joyful place," she adds, "where the words are flowing, the metaphors are original, our plot makes us laugh or cry…" and we can take pride in our work.

Another neighbor, John Stith, is a prize-winning science fiction writer and he notes his urge to write came from reading terrific books that made him say, "Wow. I wish I could do that — create something that gave other people" the joy, pleasure and happiness that those other authors provided.

Writing is also a form of playfulness. An opportunity to make things up, invent images, ideas, journeys. It is similar to what encourages people to sing, dance, paint, play guitar. These are some of the ways we express ourselves as human beings and connect with one another. "I am here and this is where I stand."

We write to share ideas, encouragement, gratitude, hope and prayers. Becoming a better writer helps us connect and communicate better with one another.

We write to be a better friend, a better citizen and to share our humanity with those around us.

If you want to be a good writer, you have to stay in shape and exercise your writing muscles; you have to write regularly. The gifted athlete stays in shape by practicing every day.

"Don't Get it Right, Get it Written"

Effective writers help us understand ourselves and our universe. They explain things, heighten consciousness, celebrate freedom, promote community, inspire, persuade, heal, entertain and outrage.

Gifted writers change how we think, dream and behave. Plato and Machiavelli changed how we understand leadership and governance. Shakespeare, Tolstoy and Orwell taught us about the human condition. Harriet Beecher Stowe, John Steinbeck, Aleksandr Solzhenitsyn and Martin Luther King, Jr. educated us about fairness, justice and humanity. Charles Darwin, Rachel Carson and Richard Feynman were scientists who transformed our thinking and behavior, just as Emily Dickinson and Seamus Heaney altered the way we see and appreciate.

Writing well is hard. The good news is that, in common with most skills and sports, one can train and prepare, practice and achieve. Like running, cooking and gardening, the more you write the more likely you'll get better. *Writing as a Performing Art* is written as a conversation — as a guide and encouragement for would-be nonfiction writers of any age. It is intentionally a more light hearted, didactic and irreverent essay than what linguists, English professors and professional grammarians provide.

Aspiring writers should commit to seven demanding activities: observing, listening, reading, critical thinking, interpreting, writing and rewriting.

Observers ask questions. They question both answers and questions. They ask "why?" and "what if?" questions as they examine everything from politics to particles. They conduct mind as well as lab experiments. One of the wonderful things about three- and four-year old children is how they frequently ask why something works this way, or why they should act that way. Creative writers and creative scientists, like curious children, are observers and questioners.

Creative people bring a spontaneity and questioning to what they hear and observe. They see things in a fresh way, noticing what is absent as well as present. Creative people embrace paradox, contradiction and juxtaposition. They freely call upon both rational and intuitive capabilities.

If you stop observing you might as well stop writing, because writing requires exploring, examining, investigating and squinting with your ears.

Writers read. It is unlikely you'll find a successful writer who isn't also a keen, avid and widely read reader. More on that later — except to note that writers begin by imitating writers they admire before gradually finding their voices. No one is a talented skier on their first outing. We fall and get up, and fall again and get up again, and try harder as we watch and imitate what others are doing. We gradually get the hang of it. It takes time, especially as one tries to learn the art of writing. That's true about writing as it is true of just about all the skills and talents we seek to master.

When we write we move from listening to asking readers to listen. Listening, observing and interpreting come first.

Write as you talk. Sound like yourself. You can't completely write as you talk; writing needs to be more succinct and disciplined than casual conversation. Still, you can use colloquial language, tell personal stories and use contractions. Spare us, however, the "you know," "uh," "like." "umm," "well-l-l" and "so." Use the language of everyday communicating and avoid erudite or "ten-dollar" phrases. Writing is sharing and conversation, always mindful of your audience.

Use as many words as it takes, and as few as you need. Use shorter rather than longer words. Use shorter instead of longer paragraphs. Let action verbs and concrete nouns do the heavy lifting. Make every word count.

Authenticity matters. Be yourself — everyone else is taken. The enemy of clear writing is being insincere or impersonal.

Clarity of thought flows from clarity of thinking. Unless you are a James Joyce or William Faulkner, simplicity is the goal.

Strive for freshness, insight, cadence and flow. Junk zombie nouns, needless adjectives, wheezy clichés, non-nutritional twinkie words, hackneyed platitudes, bromides and "double headers." The road to writer's hell is paved with adverbs, hedging, clutter and anemic phrases.

How important is it to be precise and concise? "There's not much to be said about the period," said William Zinsser, "except that most writers don't reach it soon enough."[1]

Read good writers and figure out why they succeed. The would-be writer reads the classics — Homer, Shakespeare, Cervantes, Tolstoy, Melville, Joyce, Hugo, Steinbeck and Morrison. Read first-rate magazines, newspapers and blogs. Adopt writers whose writing inspires you as role models. Collect their writings and deconstruct their style. Writers begin by imitating writers they admire. Imitate, adapt and you'll soon develop your own techniques, style and voice. Trumpeter Miles Davis suggests that, "you have to play for a while before you can play like yourself." The same is true in writing.

Part of the job of a writer is to entertain. You might achieve this by sharing anecdotes, a short personal story, a satirical note or two, outlining a paradox or by sharing surprising facts or data. Such devices can be contrived, yet the challenge is to hold your reader's interest by providing something new and fresh. "Given a choice between two travelling companions," writes William Zinsser, "and a writer is someone who asks us to travel with him — we usually choose the one who we think will make an effort to brighten the trip."[2]

When we're ill, our bodies regularly search for ways to heal; when we experience conflict, we yearn for resolution. So also with our communities and nations. Writers, at their best, help us to understand conflict and the possibilities for progress. Writers can play an invaluable role in helping us to understand, heal, and remember. They point us in the direction of resolving societal conflicts. That is the genius of writers like Harriet Beecher Stowe, John Steinbeck, Herman Melville, Nathaniel Hawthorne, Stephen Hawking and Toni Morrison. Memorable writers help us learn and laugh, to resolve conflict and to understand freedom, justice, peace and love.[3]

It's helpful to direct your writing to a single reader or at least to a distinct audience. I have a former student who became a syndicated sportswriter for the Associated Press. He intentionally crafts his stories, he says, to appeal to his mother, who has watched a game at home, as well as to the rabid sports fans who, after a major NFL game, are across the street at a boisterous sports bar. To speak simultaneously to these different audiences takes talent.

Learn how to punctuate. "Readers… have a tough job to do," notes novelist Kurt Vonnegut, "and they need all the help they can get from writers."[4] After all, readers have to decipher thousands of little notations and make sense of them. Unlike symphony musicians, they have no conductor to lead them through a work. Few phrases signal how fast or slow, or loud or soft a text is to be read. Punctuation can help. "Punctuation marks," writes Pico Iyer, "are the road signs placed along the highways of our communication — to control speeds, provide directions and prevent head-on collisions."[5]

The difference between poor writing and good writing lies in *careful revising.* Edit, recast and tighten your material. Have the guts to make cuts. Spare the reader windy generalizations and flowery prose. Writers have to devise their own rules, yet be prepared more than occasionally to bend or break them.

Research, writing, rewriting and editing require disciplined work. The more you care about your writing, the more challenging it can get. Professional writers seldom boast about the easiness of their craft.

To write well requires time, hard work and intellectual focus, the kind that seldom comes naturally. No matter how much they love it, and many love it more than anything else, writing is a craft that can be lonely, demanding and even painful.

Ernest Hemingway said writing is frustrating in part because it is something you can never do as well as it can be done. Hemingway rewrote the ending of "A Farewell to Arms" at least three dozen times before he was satisfied. He said: "There's no rule on how it is to write. Sometimes it comes easily and perfectly. Sometimes it is like drilling rock and then blasting it out with charges." "I love to write," he added, "but it has never gotten any easier to do and you can't expect it to if you keep trying for something better than you can do."[6]

Each writing project, Hemingway believed, should be a new beginning — a time to try again for something never done before or for something others have tried to do and failed. One cannot, he said, be satisfied to write in another way what already has been well written. No, it is precisely because we have known such fine writers in the past that we who write are driven out beyond where we are comfortable and to where few can help.

The joy of research and writing comes from the challenge of being out there on your own, rethinking the explored realms of life and examining the unexplored. It is scary to be out there alone, yet writing itself is one of the grand liberating human activities. Working back and forth between experience and ideas, evidence and imagination, theory and data, a writer creates, imagines and reflects. A writer with a sense of justice can remind us of who we have been, where we have failed, and who we may yet become. Writers can help vanquish lies. Great writers nourish the soul and expand our sense of what it is to be human. Recent examples have been Ray Bradbury, Toni Morrison and Margaret Atwood. Russian novelist Aleksandr Solzhenitsyn said: "A writer is no sideline judge of his fellow countrymen and contemporaries; he is equally guilty of all the evil done in his country or by his people. If his country's tanks spill blood on the streets of some alien capital, the brown stains are splashed forever on the writer's face. If, some fatal night, his trusting friend is choked to death while sleeping, the bruises from the rope are on the writer's hands."[7]

As in the mastery of any skill, writing requires tenacity. If you already know how to use time effectively, writing becomes easier, and even enjoyable. Most of us, however, are accomplished procrastinators. A writing assignment can overwhelm you if you let it. Yet, if planned carefully, it can strengthen self-discipline and sharpen your ability to manage time. Effective time management is crucial.

Outline not just your paper, but your whole project — research, writing schedule, timetable for drafts and revisions.

Be prepared to retreat to a quiet or at least comfortable place and devote several hours, days or weeks to uninterrupted, focused concentration. For extroverts, such a schedule is like being sentenced to solitary confinement. If you are going to take pride in your writing, however, you must commit to extensive reading and research, rigorous analysis and intense thought, not to mention days of writing, rewriting, revising and editing a first-rate research project requires.

Selecting a Topic

Search for a worthy topic. State it simply in a sentence or two. Your project needs focus, a point of view, an answerable question or a fresh way of considering a compelling problem. Have a purpose: inform, explain, persuade, clarify, instruct, entertain.

Avoid the perfectionist inclination to tackle only those questions that are tidy or readily answered. Attacking a trivial problem is a waste of time. Any writing project, whether a senior thesis, an opinion essay, testimony before a legislature, or a treatise on a social or scientific issue, is an opportunity to match your talents against a perplexing problem.

"Broadly speaking, academic writing is argumentative writing," write Gerald Graff and Cathy Birkenstein. "You need to enter a conversation, using what others say ... as a launching pad or sounding board for your own ideas."[8]

Many writers write in response to other writers or points of view. Sometimes this involves agreeing with earlier writers or speakers. Yet it can also involve contending that previous thinking is wrong and needs reexamination. Writing has much in common with debating. You might concede certain points, yet try to shed light — based on your research and analysis — that permits a fresh way of understanding a concept, theory or explanatory model.

Hence, in selecting a topic, you may start out seeking to confirm or disprove a particular point of view. This requires you to understand the point of view, engage it, summarize it and present your findings in the context of what others have said about it.

Be sure your topic interests you enough that you will devote the time needed for research and writing. Although few purely original ideas exist, make sure your topic is researchable and that it has not already been so researched that little or nothing remains to be added. Take care that you don't bite off more than you can chew, and don't chew more than is worth chewing. Your project has to answer "So what?" questions. Your goal is to shed new light on a problem or issue.

Curiosity spawns most writing projects: the urge to understand something better, to resolve or at least to grasp a paradox, dilemma, or set of previously unsolved, unanswered questions. My own writing often springs from questions students or others asked me, and from question-and-answer sessions. When I give an answer I am not satisfied with, I say to myself, "That good question deserves a better answer."

Always have an iPad, smart phone or pen and paper handy. Inspiration can come when you are not directly searching for it. Any type of discussion, no matter how off-topic, can inspire an idea you have not yet considered.

Perhaps something has been puzzling you, or a topic has been covered inadequately in an earlier course, or in a speech, or in a journal or a book you've read. Topics arise from discussions with friends, teachers, colleagues, parents or from your own observations in your work. Topics emerge out of internships, campaign experiences, or laboratory and field experiments. You may also be motivated by the search for truth or by outrage at hypocrisy, lies and injustice. Good writing involves telling the truth. The biblical injunction is: "Ye shall know the truth and the truth will set you free." Yet the truth can have a way of upsetting us. "Ye shall the know the truth," British writer Aldous Huxley replied, "and the truth shall make you mad." It can do both.

Researching Your Topic

As you decide on a proposed topic, ask yourself some questions about it. What do I want to say? What's the big idea? Or puzzle? Or confusion? What is it I want to discover, solve, clarify or learn more about? Why does this institution, or process or leadership theory work in its own peculiar way? Could or should it be otherwise?

How, for example, are political and economic elites held accountable? Do we need politics and politicians? When are we well-served by political leaders? How can we reconcile democracy and authority? Are changes needed in our political system? Is one political party better able to solve our problems than others? Are our economic inequalities or our inability to prevent civil and international wars the fault of governments, inadequate leadership or deficiencies in vision? Are too many governmental regulations undermining the necessary risk-taking and creative entrepreneurship needed for inventions and innovation? How much should we be funding new bio-engineering research versus breakthroughs in quantum computing?

Here's the point: Remain curious throughout your research and see if new questions and new ideas emerge out of your work. Keep an open mind about what results you are likely to find. It may be helpful to start broad and only slowly narrow your focus.

You will have to narrow your topic in accord with your time and talent. Then ask, what is the central question? Define it. Explore its origins and development. Explain its consequences. If it is a policy, process or constitutional interpretation, you may want to analyze its effect on current and future political leaders. Try to discern the underlying assumptions, agendas, and incentives of groups advocating change or the status quo. In what ways do different schools of thought define the problem differently, and why?

You will need to clarify your topic by assimilating as much material, qualitative and quantitative, as possible. Search the literature in the libraries, the internet, periodicals and available documents. You will likely discover works that already have answered, or at least addressed, parts of your topic. Explore the availability of polling or survey data that may shed light on the problem. Interviewing knowledgeable leaders or experts, and current and former public officials, may be productive. Never underestimate the talent of local librarians, especially those who are specialists with reference works, computer search technologies and government documents. They can be valuable allies.

Equally important is knowing when to stop researching and start writing. Saying you need more time to research often masks procrastination. "The temptation to read one more book or search another library shelf was always great," remarked one pragmatic young social scientist. "Investigation leads one to ask questions which demand answers. Those answers in turn breed new questions and so on until the process gets out of hand. I found it necessary to place time limits on my work. Sometimes this meant altering objectives to comply with a timetable. This was not to shortchange myself, but rather to avoid becoming paralyzed by perpetual analysis."[9]

For many people, talking about their research and writing serves as a substitute for actually focusing on the project. "Planning to write is not writing. Outlining, researching, talking to people about what you are doing, none of that," says E.L. Doctorow, "is writing. Writing is writing."[10] It is important to substantiate your claims, enlighten your reader, and put the problem in context. Remember the aphorism: "Strive for excellence yet not for perfection." And "Don't get it right — get it written." Perfectionism as well as a preoccupation with efficiency are enemies of creative expression.

Developing and Testing Hypotheses

Good writers don't just describe a problem and propose immediate solutions. You should prepare a list of possible answers to your research questions. Anticipate objections and contrary arguments. Experiment with competing or even opposing hypotheses. How does your hypothesis stand up to critical review? Ask yourself, "What if…?" Be clear about cause-and-effect relationships. Correlation, as high school teachers taught, is not the same as causation. Clarify dependent and independent variables. For example, were the leaders shaped by their background, or were they the primary shapers of events?

Anticipate the arguments of those who might disagree with your analysis; then make their argument even more powerfully than they do. Acknowledge a strong point on their side, if there is one. Then proceed to explain why your case is stronger.

Don't be constrained by the conventional wisdom of the day. Inventions, scientific breakthroughs and better answers often come only when you step outside existing ways of thinking. Economist Joseph

Schumpeter notes that progress and productivity invariably came about because of creative destruction. Innovators disrupt and upset conventional norms.[11] Disregard prevailing wisdom, ask bold questions, consider antitheticals and counterfactuals, pose fresh possibilities. Unleash your imagination.

This strategy for enumerating hypotheses is easier to suggest than to do. Record everything relevant that comes to mind, or sounds plausible. The trick is to find those bold questions and reframe them in a useful way. Contemplate juxtapositions. We are, more than we appreciate, creatures of habit and cultural conditioning. Try to discern the mind-set shifts taking place or that need to take place.[12]

At this point logical reasoning is important. You will want to test, systematically, the plausible explanations you have posed. With a bit of ingenuity you can test solutions to difficult problems without making each particular test a two- or three-year enterprise. Appreciate, however, that empirical testing and critical reasoning are indispensable to building the body of reliable knowledge needed to arrive at convincing conclusions.

Amassed information is not knowledge, merely a distant cousin. In the age of Google, YouTube and the internet, information is readily available. It's wisdom that is scarce. Information and findings are important only as intermediate phases of your research. You must make sense of what you have gathered. This step involves analysis. Writing is ultimately an interpretive process. The skilled writer makes sense of the stories, data, aspirations, myths and the symbolic as well as practical realities that shape behavior.

Students of politics, leadership and life, for example, formulate theories about the "why" and the "so what" of political life and governance. Aristotle called the study of leadership and governance the "queen of sciences" and classified city-states according to their political structures, making predictions about how different structures would lead to different outcomes. His goal was to help us to live better lives. Plato examined the need for enlightened leaders and the responsibilities of wise, virtuous and informed leaders. Machiavelli, in "The Prince," prescribed how rulers should govern to maximize their power to provide for homeland security and prosperity. Thomas Hobbes, Alexander Hamilton,

Thomas Jefferson and James Madison were political theorists interested in formulating governing arrangements that would balance liberty and order, responsibility and leadership. Those who drafted the U.S. Constitution in the summer of 1787 in Philadelphia acted as political philosophers and political architects. They merged experience and theory in the formation of practical political institutions.

Social scientists study patterns of politics, patterns of leadership, and the exercise of power and authority, just as physical scientists study atoms, photons, particles, genes, rocks, and stars. They describe things with the intent of understanding them. Understanding can lead to explanations, explanations can lead to predictive models, and predictions can generate theory.

We search for the predictable to discover, to describe, and, if possible, to verify the basic laws of politics, humanity and matter. Although Plato's "Republic" and Aristotle's "Politics" showed the way, we are still learning how to understand human behavior and still striving to explore and understand the universe.

Just as money is the mother's milk of politics and campaigns, *evidence* is the well-spring of convincing writing. Evidence means furnishing proof, and verifiable data. Readers will justifiably ask: Did the writer back up the thesis? Is there evidence? Is the evidence clearly backed by logic, examples, data or supporting material? Evidence, evidence, evidence. What will convince readers you have made a strong case? The scientific method requires that experiments can be replicated to verify similar findings or precise measurements. This may not be possible or even necessary on every project yet providing evidence is your responsibility when you are asking readers to think anew about an old problem or a new question.

Although others have already written about most topics you will tackle, don't be discouraged. Your challenge is to examine the problem with a fresh eye. Approach it from another angle. Place it in a different, and perhaps a contemporary, context. Try to find new linkages and suggest alternative relevant explanations. The challenge of research and writing is to raise appropriate questions, generate original data, evidence or findings that point in promising directions.

Beginning to Write

Novelist Somerset Maugham joked that "there are three rules for writing a novel. Unfortunately, no one knows what they are."[13] Although the same may be true for non-fiction, here are some practical suggestions:
- Prepare a paragraph or two to focus your objectives.
- Outline your project.
- Know your audience and what is important for them as well as what should be important to them.
- Cultivate your inner ear.
- Write honestly.
- Write to convince.
- Adopt a working title.
- Revise, revise, revise.

Outlining and Focus

Is it important to know where you are going? If you don't know where you're going, says a proverb, you will doubtless end up somewhere else. The moral is important. In the past, you may have sat down at your computer and produced a first draft you thought was a final product. Your essay may have been put together by cutting and pasting odd descriptions and definitions and tagging on a rough conclusion. This is boneheaded.

Write an outline to organize your argument in logical order. Prepare a simple one-page statement of purpose to clarify your objectives. What do you intend to do? Why are you writing on this topic? Who is your audience? What's the problem? What is your main theme? What answers are you looking for? Write in sentence form each major point needed to support your thesis. Jot down, under each sentence, the evidence you will use to support your central points.

As you review and revise your outline, you will want to ask yourself more questions. What are my major points or most telling evidence? What are my weak points? Why do I care about this topic? Will the conclusion flow smoothly from the body of the essay? Have I jumped to conclusions? Will the essay persuade or offer a provocative way of seeing something?

An outline is merely a guide. It is a way of dividing a subject into its major points and subpoints. As you do more research and get into your writing, your initial outline will change. The best outlines evolve and become more focused. Don't let your outline control you; alter it to serve your goals. Still, "to get anywhere, one first has to start. And a good way to start the outline is to jot down quickly … the ideas you have about your topic, asking what there is of interest that you want to pass along to the reader."[14] Your outline is in part a plan, in part a reflection of information you have gathered, and a way of arranging your material and interpretive analysis in a logical order. Outlines are essential. They help avoid writer's block, affirm you have something to say and allow you to see how one idea logically leads to another. They organize your schedule.

Watch out for overwriting. Many people nowadays are conditioned to writing in chatty, unstructured email, texting and tweeting styles.

Computers and social media devices encourage people to write more, not necessarily better.

One report found college students submit essays that are longer, yet not better written than those in the past. "Worse, many students do not revise or even proofread their work, relying instead on software to check spelling and grammar."[15]

Spell-checks are no substitute for careful proofreading. For example, they often don't catch punctuation mistakes or differences between such words as "principle" and "principal" or "capitol" and "capital." No computer can make bad writing good.

If computers help overcome writer's block by making it easy to pour out ideas, then editing becomes even more important.

Writing Honestly

Once you have sketched an outline, it's time to put your ideas into words. Try "shotgun" writing, freestyle brainstorming, thinking in terms of blocks or chunks of ideas. Your first inclination with words is often what you really mean. Don't expect to get the vocabulary or flow exactly right on the first try. Downplay spelling and grammar rules at this stage. Concentrate on getting your ideas down in any way you can. Writing technically correct prose about irrelevant ideas is a waste of talent and energy. Keep focused on key concepts.

It's OK to be sloppy. Make a mess. Who cares? Wrong words and imperfect writing are perfectly acceptable and an understandable prelude in your drafting stages. Allow your ideas to begin to take shape. Thinking is far more important than error-free writing. Later, you can get your ideas in more concise and stylish form. "If you are like most people, you can't do much precise thinking until you have committed to paper at least a rough sketch of your initial ideas," writes Sylvan Barnet. "Later you can push and polish your ideas into shape, perhaps even deleting all of them and starting over, but it's easier to improve your ideas once you see them in front of you than it is to do the job in your head. On paper one word leads to another; in your head one word often blocks another."[16]

Each of us writes with a distinctive flavor and voice. Be yourself. Write from the heart as well as the mind. Good writing is about telling the truth as you understand it. Some stylists advise writers to place themselves in the background. They contend, with some justification, that writing and talking are different things. A speaker, for example, has a rapport with listeners and can take into account what they already know. Formal writing and putting yourself in the background will work for many. It is required if you are writing for the Yale Law Review or the New England Journal of Medicine. But most of us will be better served by writing conversationally. Voice reveals character and passion.

If you want to read writers who inject their voice and passion in their narratives, try: Edward Abbey's "Desert Solitaire: A Season in the Wilderness" (1968), Anthony Bourdain's "Kitchen Confidential" (2018 edition), Ayn Rand's "Atlas Shrugged" (1957), J.D. Salinger's "Catcher in the Rye" (1951) or J.D. Vance's "Hillbilly Elegy" (2016). Abbey takes you into the desert, brings it alive and bares his soul about what he loves and what he hates. Bourdain, who was a celebrity chef, takes you into kitchens where he worked and shares his joys about delicious food as well as his warnings about the underbelly of even the most chic restaurants. Salinger's classic lives because of his irresistibly irreverent Holden Caulfield and Caulfield's caustic, surly and preppy depictions of his schools, family, friends and New York.

Professionals have long debated formal versus colloquial writing. There is a place for both. But readability increases when writers write in the first-person pronoun. "Write as you talk" is encouraged. Abraham Lincoln wrote by ear and liked to read his speech drafts aloud to anyone who would listen. His attitude was that "if it sounds all right, I just let it pass." Writers with a good ear are advantaged just as jazz players are. The playwright Damon Runyon and the novelist Gertrude Stein used little punctuation to get readers to listen to their narrators as if they were speaking. Try it.

For a splendid example of conversational, instructive yet surprisingly entertaining writing, see John D. Cox's "Weather for Dummies" (2021).

When we were youngsters, we had little difficulty sounding the way we felt. Most children speak and write with an authentic voice. But adults have to work harder to achieve the same simple, direct honesty. Writing with no voice is lifeless, mechanical and wooden because it lacks rhythm and individuality. Peter Elbow explains that:

> Most people's writing lacks voice because they stop so often in mid-sentence and ponder, worry, or change their minds about which word to use or which direction to go in …
>
> Writing with *voice* is writing into which someone has breathed. It has fluency, rhythm, and liveliness that exist naturally in speech of most people when they are enjoying a conversation.
>
> Writing with *real voice* has the power to make you pay attention and understand.[17]

Writing to Convince and Persuade

A writer's job is both to pull your readers along and to educate them. Even better: to persuade your readers into rethinking their positions.

"Convince" and "persuade" are often used interchangeably, but technically, they are different. You persuade someone to *do* something and convince someone *of* something.

The first job of a writer, especially an opinion writer, is to know your audience. And to listen and understand their opinions and biases, hopes and fears. Readers want writers to understand them — an obvious challenge for the writer who, in most instances, has never met them.

Here are tips from a veteran New York Times editor whose job was to accept, reject and edit guest opinion columns in the Times.

- Know what has already been written and find a different angle.
- Address a problem and offer a solution.
- Get to your main idea quickly.
- Clichés and jargon will doom you.
- Avoid the obvious.

- Avoid being self-promotional.
- Target your audience by connecting to its values and aspirations.
- Share something memorable, adding surprising or unappreciated facts.
- Readers like to be informed of the socially accepted consensus, but may be open to contrarian ideas if presented in a honest and humble way.
- The use of graphs, tables and charts can help readers overcome misperceptions.
- Readers love stories. Stories draw people in and engage them.
- When in doubt, keep it short.

"There's one big problem," adds editor Trish Hall, "with saying how long or how short articles should be: It just depends. You know how long you can keep readers? Until they're bored. Sometimes they're bored before the end of the first sentence. Sometimes they read 3,000 words and wish there were more. It's all about pulling along your readers. If you're not telling a story with all the classic ingredients that hold people — love, war, sex, conflict, tragedy — then keep it short."[18]

Revising

Starting to write is the most difficult part of writing for some people. For others, rewriting, revising and editing are more taxing. Rewriting is the essence of writing. If you are not already relentless about editing, erasing and discarding unnecessary words: change. Ask yourself *"can I write it more concisely?"* If it is possible to cut a word, delete it.

Ernest Hemingway jokingly called his lean, economical and understated writing style his "iceberg theory" of writing. Others called it the "omission theory." If a word didn't add anything, Hemingway gave it the deep-freeze treatment.

A "New Simplicity" movement in England once crusaded against using too many adverbs, metaphors, polysyllables, subordinate clauses and their cousins. Keep this in mind, yet not as a rigid rule. Your own style and voice and inner editor will lead you.

James Michener wrote wonderful best-sellers about places like Hawaii, Colorado and the Chesapeake Bay, yet he described himself as a talented rewriter rather than a gifted writer.

One technique for learning to revise and edit your work is to "use the knife" on other people's writings.

It's easier to find the flaws and what doesn't work in a colleague's drafts. Exchange papers. Read a classmate's or colleague's paper and ask them to proof and critique your work. Others can see more clearly what doesn't make sense or doesn't flow. It is relatively painless to delete and mark up "their" prose. "Once you get comfortable wielding the knife and seeing blood on the floor, it turns out to be easier to wield it on yourself."[19]

Here's an exercise of putting your editor's knife to work. Abraham Lincoln's Gettysburg Address is one of the sacred documents in American history. It took Lincoln just two or three minutes to deliver the 272 words he had titled "Remarks." Pulitzer Prize winner John McPhee assigned his Princeton writing students to edit Lincoln's masterpiece.

When I first heard of his exercise, I thought it was crazy, even sacrilegious. Still, I tried it with my students, permitting them to substitute an occasional word or phrase for transitions as they went about their cutting. My students, presumably like McPhee's, were able to cut Lincoln's "Remarks" in half and sometimes down to 75 or 100 words — without losing its essence. Some of them even improved Lincoln. The lesson is: if you are bold enough to use the delete button on Lincoln, you can be bold enough to put your own writing on a diet.

Urban legend has it that Hemingway was once challenged to compose a six-word short story. He promptly, so the story goes, jotted on his napkin: "For sale: Baby shoes, never worn." This may be a made-up tale, yet it makes a point.

Pulitzer Prize-winning poet Stanley Kunitz was asked if he had ever written a poem he thought perfect. He said he had deceived himself on occasion into thinking so. "But," he added, "I no more expect a poem to be perfect than I expect a life to be perfect. The two are interwoven and inseparable. And if it's humans, the likeliness of perfection is so remote we might as well forget about it. One does the best one can and then one revises it. Then you revise it again. And then you publish it. And you see new flaws and then you try again. That's the life in art."[20]

How many drafts get you to the ideal draft? This too depends. Good writing often begins with problematic first efforts. Anne Lamott talks about a friend who considers the first draft as "the down draft — you just get it down. The second draft is the up draft — you fix it up. You try to say what you have to say more accurately. And the third draft is the dental draft, where you check every tooth to see if it's loose or cramped or decayed or ..."[21]

Somehow "the dental draft" doesn't sound as if it should be a writer's ultimate or even penultimate draft. But it all depends on each writer, the intended audience and, of course, on how much time you have to revise, polish and shine your would-be masterpiece.

Begin the process of revising by reading your early efforts aloud to yourself, your friends or anyone you can get to listen. When you read aloud, you hear and see things you otherwise may be unable to discern. The tongue may trip over an out-of-place or incorrect word. The ear catches errors of substance and style the eye often misses. Reading aloud also stresses what is important. An effective sentence is partly a matter of cadence and rhythm. Abraham Lincoln succeeded with precision and elegance, and also with his uncommon vernacular ease and rhythmical virtuosity.[22]

Journalist James J. Kilpatrick urged us to "sound out" our sentences and suggests that if a sentence lacks cadence, it collapses like an overcooked soufflé. Essential to good writing is a good ear. Listen to your prose. Cultivate the inner ear. "The writer who learns the knack of balance or of deliberate imbalance; the writer who understands how to quicken his tempo with short words, quick darting words that smack and jab; the writer who learns to slow his composition with soft and languorous convolutions; the writer who practices the trick of sentence endings, striving deliberately for syllables that are accented in a particular way, for the long vowel sound or the short — such a writer is on his way toward mastery of a marvelous tool."[23]

Editing means figuring out what you want to say and saying it. Just as effective leaders avoid wasting people's time, effective writers make sure they have something to say and avoid boring their readers with clutter. After a draft or two or three, you'll want to get it clear in your head and then rewrite it in the most accurate way.

Editing has a lot in common with gardening: trimming, pruning, weeding. Just as most gardens grow weedy, writing can become wordy.

Selecting Words Carefully

The most common writing deficiency is an overly casual approach to the use of words. "Use the right word," Mark Twain said, "not its distant cousin." Ask yourself: *What is it I'm trying to say? Why am I using this word? Does it look right? Does it sound right? Is there a better, fresher way to say it? Is it clear, direct, brief and bold? Can one word suffice for the two or three now used?*

"Vigorous writing is concise. A sentence should contain no unnecessary words, for the same reason that a drawing should have no unnecessary lines and a machine no unnecessary parts," advise William Strunk, Jr., and E.B. White. "This requires not that the writer make all his sentences short, or that he avoid all detail and treat his subjects only in outline, but that every word tell."[24] Strunk and White set a high bar for us. Most of us will never be so talented that every word tells, yet it's an aspiration.

In addition to using accurate words, try using familiar, simple, unadorned words. Simplicity increases readability. Complexity, unorthodox usages, needless adjectives, transitional adverbs, excessive use of semicolons, hyphens and abstract nouns diminish flow.

Strive for lean writing. Avoid jargon, pedantry, clichés and "out-of-town" or foreign phrases designed to show off erudition. Arrogance pervades the work of certain scholars. The greatest discovery in history is useless if no one understands what it means. One of my students summed up obfuscation perfectly: "It is a cardinal sin of so-called 'teachers' to write and talk so their students cannot understand them — I hate that." There is nothing wrong with using an exotic word now and then if it is the best one to describe what you're talking about, yet if your writing is aimed at a lay audience, use words ordinary readers will understand.

"The obscurity that characterizes professional economic prose does not derive from the difficulty of the subject" wrote prize-winning economist and bestselling author John Kenneth Galbraith. "It is the result of incomplete thought; or it reflects a priestly desire to differentiate one's self from the plain world of the layman; or it stems from a fear of having one's inadequacies found out."[25]

The job of the writer is to have something to say, to say it as clearly as possible and to make sense of complexity. Many important ideas are complex or have paradoxical aspects to them. Writers put things in perspective and try, with appropriate nuance, to simplify. We are expected to uncomplicate the complicated and make sense of things for our readers. James Joyce is an ingenious exception. He was a masterful complexifier who flouted the rules and wrote allusive, flowery and stream-of-consciousness characterizations. He is said to have known 17 languages, and he quoted--with no translation-- from many of them. He reveled in word play, puns, parody, literary and classical references and was a linguistic exhibitionist. His books were shunned, banned and burned — yet read, read, and read. But imitating the gifted Joyce won't work for most of us.

Language is a subjective matter. Substituting too many short, conventional words for unusual ones can devitalize your writing. A trade-off exists: simplicity on the one hand, the use of unusual words on the other. Excessive editing can make language drab, commonplace and lifeless. Long paragraphs and sacrilegious punctuation can work for gifted writers like Joyce, William Faulkner and Toni Morrison. Long and unfamiliar words sometimes work as well. For example, a few writers use the word "hornswoggled" and make it work. One acquaintance, however, used "durational expectancy," a phrase that didn't work for me. New Yorkers can say and write "*Fuhgeddaboutdit!*" or "*Oy veh*" and we get it. Occasionally, unfamiliar words or phrases fit the meaning best or serve the rhythm of a sentence.

50 Pet Peeve Words

Everyone has pet peeves. Some of us have pet peeve words. They are pretentious "highbrow" words that slow down reading. Or words so overused they are annoying. Here are my nominations for words that are hard on the eye or hard on the ear. Make your own list and please share them.

Aforementioned	Holistic
Albeit	Impactful
Aperture	Inauthentic
Approbation	Inauspicious
Cavil	Inchoate
Chthonic	Irregardless
Conundrum	Latitudian
Contextualize	Mandations
Correlative	Monetizable
Decisionmakingwise	Officialese
Desuetude	Paradigmatic
Desultory	Performative
Downloadable	Perspectival
Dysphemism	Pointillism
Egregious	Positivity
Entymological	Prioritization
Eponymous	Prodigality

Eschatological	Provenance
Eschew	Relatable
Existential	Slitheriness
Fatigable	Tentacular
Finalize	Unputdownable
Gubernatorial	Untoward
Hashtaggable	Winningest
Hermeneutic	Worryingly

Here are a few additions suggested by former New York Times editor Trish Hall. She liked to delete these tired or jargon words and phrases and I gladly add them to my pet peeve list: pivot, drill down, incentivize, end users, win-win, scalable, synergize, on the same page, think outside the box.[26]

As a bonus, or perhaps a punishment, let me share 10 "choice Joyce" words from my reading of Joyce's acclaimed "Ulysses": adiapane, auspicated, deluciated, dunductetymudecolored, farrangionous, jollification, lycopdium, objurgations, gumbenjamin and exhibitionististicity. Joyce has a surprise word on nearly every page, sometimes in another language.

Let's Hear it for Everyday Words

It's hard to see any advantage in long or fancy words when a simple, everyday word will do. Thus, choose "she said" rather than "she opined," "he read" rather than "he perused," "she lives at …" rather than "she resides at …" Choose "he ranked states" rather than "he enumerated states." Use "before," not "prior to." Avoid writing "in order to." As a general rule, use the Anglo-Saxon word rather than its Latinate cousin.

An Associated Press handbook suggests replacing the longer words on the left with the shorter words on the right:[27]

Ameliorate → improve
Approximately → about
Commence → begin
Deactivate → close, shut off
Endeavor → try
Implement → carry out
In consequence of → because
Initiate → begin
Methodology → method
Objective → aim, goal
Proliferation → spread

Purchase → buy
Remuneration → pay
Replicate → repeat
Socialize → mingle, meet
Underprivileged → poor
Utilize → use

Writing and rewriting are a constant and never-ending search for what you want to say, and saying it as clearly and persuasively as you can. One sees adverbs and redundant words that can be deleted. Better transition sentences may be needed. Polish introductory sentences to make them telegraph where you are headed. Remember there are few ideas in any discipline that cannot, with effort, be expressed in clear writing. Understand, too, that it is impossible to conclude everything as you wrap up your final draft.

Let Verbs Do the Heavy Lifting

Use short words, short sentences, and short paragraphs. Less is more. Carefully selected verbs and nouns seldom need adjectives and adverbs to amplify their meaning. "The adverb," novelist Stephen King contends, "is not your friend."

Strong verbs (verbs that show action) infuse sentences with protein and life-giving nectar. Writers can accomplish more with a carefully chosen, vivid verb than with a truckload of adjectives. A common verb offense is using the lame verb forms *"there is," "there are," "it is"* and *"it seems to be"* where the word *"it"* is impersonal and has no referent. Good writers avoid "to be" verbs. People fall into the habit of using these out of laziness. They weaken most sentences and can almost always be replaced by more telling verbs.

Further, using strong verbs contributes to word economy. Take the following simple example: "There is one legislator who writes most of the committee's bills and reports." Remove bland words: *there, is, who, of* and *the*. Now your sentence reads: *"One legislator writes most committee bills and reports.*" The new sentence is five words shorter and has a fiber verb as its engine.

Active verbs make for vital sentences. An active verb has the person performing the action as its subject, as in "*I am voting,*" or "*She leads her team.*" A passive verb is a form of the "to be" family plus the past participle, as in "*The group is being led by Heather,*" or "*The election results have been counted.*" Try: "*Heather leads her team,*" and "*They tallied the votes.*"

The active voice stresses the one doing something, and provides pace and movement in reading. Active verbs push, strike, carry and persuade. "Joe led the discussion" is strong. "The discussion was led by Joe" is limp. The passive voice shifts the focus from who to what's being done and makes for sluggish reading. It slows the pace and usually requires more words. "The active voice strikes like a boxer moving forward in attack," writes Theodore M. Bernstein. "The passive voice parries while backpedaling."[28] Recall Henry David Thoreau's advice about how to live: simplify, simplify, simplify. This applies to writing, as well.

Clear, lean thinking is usually the key to clear, lean writing. Keep complicated constructions to a minimum. The "secret of good writing is to strip every sentence to its cleanest components," writes William Zinsser. "Every word that serves no function, every word that could be a short word, every adverb which carries the same meaning that is already in the verb, every passive construction that leaves the reader unsure of who is doing what — these are the thousand and one adulterants that weaken the strength of a sentence."[29]

Use Qualifiers Sparingly

Be bold. Be definite. Say it in positive form. Take a stand. Be careful using qualifiers: *it seems, it appears, very, quite, rather, usually, mostly, generally, a lot, all right, some, often, various, frequently, probably, apparently, seemingly, basically* and *essentially*. Banish: *somewhat unique, very unique* or *almost unique*. "Unique" is an absolute adjective; *unique* is unique.

Avoid using *pretty, really, sort of* and similar words as qualifiers of intensity in formal writing. Be careful not to confuse qualifiers of size (huge, tremendous) with qualifiers of intensity (significant, important). Be cautious in using words like *every, never, always, all* and *so*. I love the Urban Dictionary riff on the word "so": "The first word of any answer given by a know-it-all douchebag, said to give the effect that they were already speaking when you asked your question or requested their opinion, in order to feign superiority or to imply that they knew what you wanted to know before you inquired." (urbandictionary.com)

Restrain the temptation to hedge with *possibly, if only, moreover, furthermore, the fact that, it is my* understanding, I would argue, it is believed that, it is sometimes said that, due to, on one hand, however, that which, that is to say, notwithstanding* and *to the contrary notwithstanding.* A qualifier is necessary, of course, if a statement or partial evidence is open to doubt; hence an occasional *perhaps, reportedly* or *substantially* has to be used.

"Many writers," writes psycholinguist Steven Pinker, "cushion their prose with wads of fluff that imply that they are not willing to stand behind what they are saying." Among his disliked hedging are: *partially, presumably, so to speak, somewhat, to some extent* and *to a certain degree.* "Writers," he adds, "acquire the hedge habit to conform to the bureaucratic imperative that's abbreviated as 'CYA.' Words I spell out as 'Cover your Anatomy'!"[30]

Why be "sort of" strong? Be strong. Skip the rather in "rather seriously" and "rather strong." "Strong" and "seriously" do the job. Try using "expert" rather than billing someone as a "top expert." Why can't cable television introduce "the news" rather than labelling everything as "breaking news"?

Good writers accentuate the positive and downplay the negative. Although we can't convert every negative to an affirmative, consider these translations:[31]

not many	→	few
not the same	→	different
does not have	→	lacks
did not stay	→	left
did not consider	→	ignored
did not accept	→	rejected
not possible	→	impossible
not able	→	unable
not certain	→	uncertain

Avoid Doubleheaders

Avoid paired words often called "doubleheaders:" *beck and call, bound and determined, safe and sound, fresh and new, clear and simple, nuts and bolts, full and complete, first and foremost, hope and trust, each and every, fair and just.* See if one word will say it. "Lawyers love paired words with related meanings, like null and void, part and parcel, aid and abet, sum and substance, irrelevant and immaterial," laments Rene Cappon. But these doubleheaders are "kissing cousins of redundancies."[32]

Edit clutter. Strike *of all* in "*First of all.*" Replace *end results* with *result, serious crisis* with *crisis, true facts* with *facts, personal beliefs* with *beliefs, free gift* with *gift, single-most* with *single, new record* with *record, at this point in time* with *now, considering the fact that* with *because,* and *beware of the fact that* with *know.* Delete *together* in "The team gathered together." Delete the *very* in "Susan is a very strong leader." The word *very* weakens the word *strong*, just as the word *pretty* weakens the word *red* in "The brick building is pretty red." [More later on the use of very.] "He would claim that running is easier than swimming" is better written, "He claims running is easier than swimming." "My visit to China will always be remembered by me" is improved to, "I'll remember my visit to China." Use *if* instead of *in the event that*. Use *since* for *in view of the fact that*. Use *thus* instead of *thusly*, *now* instead of *currently* or *presently*, *met* instead of *held a meeting*, *agreed* instead of *reached an agreement*, *because* instead of *due to the fact that*. Use *to* instead of *in order to* and *return* for *return back*.

Good writers delete redundant words. A redundant phrase implicates and needlessly thickens a sentence. Here, thanks to the "Oxford American Writer's Thesaurus,"[33] are examples of how to delete superfluous words:

<del>absolutely</del> essential
<del>completely</del> random
each <del>and every</del>
<del>fellow</del> teammates
<del>just</del> recently
<del>new</del> innovation
<del>old</del> proverb
spelled out <del>in detail</del>
<del>temporary</del> reprieve

<del>ultimate</del> conclusion
whether <del>or not</del>
<del>actual</del> evidence
<del>close</del> proximity
<del>root</del> cause
<del>safe</del> haven
<del>totally</del> destroyed
worst <del>ever</del>
fall <del>down</del>

Avoid tired, overused words. Instead of saying a point is *important, exciting* or *obvious*, make it so. If you are clear, you do not have to use *clearly, plainly, doubtless, actually* or *most assuredly*. Most readers tire of the anemic phrases: *needless to say, world-class, bottom line* and *that said*. I dislike: *so here's the bottom line, and here's the thing* and *at the end of the day*. Colorless words and phrases make even the freshest prose stale. The joy of writing is getting it right in as lively a way as possible.

Beware of clichés. They can't be completely avoided, yet they are usually lame. Examples: *few and far between, busy as a bee, barking up the wrong tree, axe to grind, six of one, half a dozen of the other, water under the bridge, pulled no punches, this is where the rubber meets the road, it isn't rocket science, game-changer, move the needle*. Use them sparingly if you have to and shun them when they substitute for precise thinking.[34]

Also, avoid telling us what you are about to tell us. Just say it. Impeach wordy introductions such as *it is interesting to note that, also important is the fact that, therefore it seems that, the fact of the matter is that ... What I would like to say is... I would at this juncture in my paper..., it is now time for this writer* to admit her own..., the thesis here is that..., and the point I want to make here is that we..., be that as it may... and in conclusion. Eliminate history tells us. Junk the phrase further research is needed. It always is.

Curb phrasing that makes repetition necessary to keep the sentence on track; strings of nouns depending on one another; prepositions, conjunctions and adverbial expressions made up of two or more words: with reference to, in conjunction with, in terms of, in the event that, in the nature of, as to whether, in lieu of, in relation to. Often a single, one-syllable word will do: in, with, for.

Beware of zombie nouns. Nominalizations (sorry for jargon) are abstract nouns formed from verbs or adjectives, often through the addition of suffix endings, such as ism, ity, ance and ian. Think obfuscation, fortuitousness, suggestion or globalization. Helen Sword calls them zombie nouns because, she says, they cannibalize active verbs and suck the energy out of sentences.[35]

Her advice is to avoid them or rewrite a sentence so the verb, preferably a vivid verb, does the work. Thus, prefer decided to make a decision. Prefer suggest to offer a suggestion.

I cringed when I heard these zombie verbs: "He was ratioed," shared a television guest commentator. He meant that a talked-about presidential candidate was getting more negatives than positives on Twitter and Facebook social commentary. Another zombie verb: "He wasn't Mirandized." This meant the arrested person wasn't read his legal Miranda rights. Finally, "The legislator is worried about being primaried."

Nouns converted to verbs make for clunky reading. They lumber across the page like lifeless zombies.

Spare Us "Twinkies"

A "twinkie" word takes its meaning from junk food, which has little or no nutrition. Nominations for twinkie or bubblegum awards are *to say the least, literally, interesting, nice, meaningful, exciting, hopefully, key, insightful, great, there are, there is, there were, and so forth, and the like, and so on, crucial, landmark, drastic, stimulating, sensitive, things, as a matter of fact, be that as it may* and *parameter*. Omit *with reference to, in the nature of*. Excessive use has spoiled these until they've become hollow.

My favorite put-down of a twinkie is the tale of the grocery store checkout clerk telling the poet: Have a *nice* day. The poet's response: "No thanks, I have other plans."

Avoid jargon. Adding *-wise* and *-ize* to the end of words may be fashionable, but it undermines clarity. The suffix *-wise* has a place in established forms like *clockwise, otherwise* and *likewise*, but adding it to most nouns makes for tortuous prose. Made-up words like *politicswise, P.R-wise, marketwise, streetwise, leadershipwise, policywise, datawise, wordwise* and *mediawise* are rude to the ear and eye.

Although *finalize, prioritize, divisionalize, definitize, analogize* and *bureaucratize* are formed by the same process that created the acceptable *popularize, concertize* and *modernize,* best to skip them. Better words can be employed. For *finalize,* try *complete, conclude* or *end.* Also avoid trendy words like *scenario, input, interface, impact, effectuate, bottom line, cool, drill, watershed, prioritization* and *awesome.*

See if you can drop *overexaggerate, it goes without saying, by the way, irregularly, charmingly, redoubtable, the thing is* and *the point is.*

Be Correct

For most of us, English is the primary language we'll use when writing. Learn its rules of grammar and syntax. Learn to spell. I'm mildly dyslexic, and prize the saying that only creative people know how to spell a word three ways. I learned I had this challenge only when our son was diagnosed with this condition. Our dyslexic's mock cheer is: "Dyslexics of the world, untie!" Still, when in doubt, I look it up. Because I'm dyslexic and "old school," I keep a dictionary and thesaurus at my writing desk alongside my spell-check device. I also try to have someone proofread my drafts.

Dyslexics also typically, like me, have a challenge differentiating right from left. Don't expect us to know leeward from starboard, or aft from port — at least quickly. We have trouble accurately grasping certain numbers such as 3, 5 and 8. We can also mix up months.

Here are words that, even in my old age, I still have to doublecheck because they are hard for me and, I suspect, a few others, to spell: February, tomorrow, surprise, calendar, judgment, irrelevant, laboratory, accommodate, ninety, independence, perseverance, affect vs. effect, lose vs. loose, chose vs. choose, stationary vs. stationery, desert vs. dessert, whose vs. who's, farther vs. further. I doubt I'm alone on many of these.

Still, spelling and grammar mistakes, at least in your final draft, imply a lazy writer who is indifferent to the reader. Worse, by calling attention to themselves, bad spelling or grammar disrupts the flow of ideas. Readers won't stick with a careless writer.

On the Other Hand: Dueling with the Grammar Police

Dyslexics hate spelling bees. A close runner-up were classes devoted to diagramming sentences.

I don't remember most of the grammar rules we were supposed to learn, even though I took several years of Latin, Greek and French, as well as the standard English courses. All I remember is sharing the complaint that those people — especially teachers — who circled our typos and grammatical delinquencies were "losers" who were not trying hard enough to understand what we were saying.

Jazz musicians improvise without knowing how to read music. Duke Ellington, in the early 1940s, wrote "it don't mean a thing if it ain't got that swing." He added, "it makes no difference if it's sweet or it's hot. Just give that rhythm ev'rything you got." Although it may be cute to say rules are made to be bent, creative people — as well as we dyslexics — don't let friends become imprisoned by rules.

A writer worried about conjunctions, contractions, correlatives, determiners, partitives, concession clauses, dangling participles and the proper usages of transitive and intransitive verbs may well procrastinate instead of writing. The goal is to write well enough to explain, persuade, convince--to take it to the house/audience. If it looks and sounds good, it probably is good. Leave it and click: "next."

Rules are meant to provide guidance and clarity. Yet rules change. And several traditional old-school rules can be broken. Theodore M. Bernstein, longtime editor at The New York Times, writes that as times have changed the rules of language have become more relaxed. Old taboos, bugbears and strictures have been modified. The stylist E.B. White allowed that "some infinitives seem to improve on being split." Calvin Trillin suggested, "As far as I'm concerned 'whom' is a word that was invented to make everyone sound like a butler." George Orwell famously shared a few rules for writing, yet wonderfully added: "Break any of these rules sooner than writing anything outright barbarous."

Here are ideas about "bending the rules":
- It's OK to begin a sentence with a conjunction (*but, and ,or*). Just don't overdo it.
- It's OK to split an infinitive if this makes a sentence more readable.

- It's OK to use the first person singular (*I, me, my*) in anything but the most formal writing assignment.
- One-sentence paragraphs are as acceptable as long paragraphs. One-sentence paragraphs are more common in journalism than in formal writing. Let readability and pace be your guide.
- When it comes to using punctuation marks (commas, colons, semicolons, hyphens, etc.), aim for readable flow. Semicolons are used less frequently nowadays. Forgo the Oxford comma (used after the next-to-the-last word in a series, just before your final *and*), unless it mucks up the clarity of your sentence. Those in the Oxford comma camp defend their use as a means to avoid ambiguity — and they are occasionally correct.
- *"Whom"* is a dying word. We remember it in Hemingway's "For Whom the Bell Tolls," and "*to whom it may concern*," yet for most of us, *whom* will usually sound wrong, even if it is right. *Who* will usually sound right, even when it may be wrong. Why not just avoid "whoming."

- It's OK to use contractions. We use them in everyday conversation. Again, it depends on our audience, yet conversational writing is readable writing.
- Slang and colloquialisms can add spice and variety, as well as voice. But slang should be used with moderation. Most people today understand *"hood"* as shorthand for *neighborhood*, or expressions such as *"my bad"* or *"homey"* or *"I have your back."* But many readers will dislike *"the middle finger,"* the f-word, ethnic slights or some of the words rap artists use. What works in one community or culture may not in another. Know your audience. You have to decide how appropriate it is to use trending words.
- Shakespeare added hundreds of new words and phrases to the language. Dictionaries add hundreds every year. Every new technology generates a new vocabulary: *Uber, selfie, sofa-surfing, bitcoin, doxing, crypto-bully, zooming, fintech, biohacking, Minecraft, like*s, *Waymo Netflix and metaverse* are now embedded in our everyday conversations.

- And as New Yorker editor Mary Norris writes, "You cannot legislate language. ... Prohibition never worked, right? Not for booze and not for sex and not for words. And yet no one wants to be pummeled constantly by four-letter words. If we are going to use them, let's use them right."[36]
- Modern writers playfully mix up nouns and verbs. The verb *repurpose* comes from the noun *purpose*, the verb *task* from the noun *task*. *Doxing* derives from *documents*. But beware the plague of zombie words.
- Numbers are traditionally written out rather than presented as numerals. Yet the acclaimed Toni Morrison begins her "Beloved" with these two sentences:
  "*124 was spiteful. Full of a baby's venom.*"
  The haunted house at 124 sticks with the reader in this majestic work precisely because it is shown as numerals.

The best way to learn the rules of grammar and effective style is to read savvy authors. Read Willa Cather, Anna Quindlen, Lewis Thomas and Michael

Lewis, and journalists like David Brooks, Jason Gay or Peggy Noonan.

Celebrated writers often seem to enjoy playing with the traditional rules and going rogue with grammar rules. Here are some famous writers who chose, like Frank Sinatra's song, to "do it their way":

- William Faulkner's "Absalom, Absalom" begins with a 123-word sentence with just one comma. Faulkner flouted regular punctuation guidelines. It made for tough reading. His advice for tackling his prose: "Read it four times." Loyal readers did.
- Jack Kerouac's "On the Road" is one 400-page paragraph. One.
- Norman Mailer's "Harlot's Ghost" is 1,100 pages with no semicolons.
- Herman Melville's "Moby-Dick" has thousands of semicolons.
- Toni Morrison's "Beloved" has sections where she makes up her own punctuation and has paragraphs run on for several pages.
- William Burrough's "Naked Lunch" gets carried away with excessive ellipses and addiction descriptions.

- Hunter S. Thompson's "Fear and Loathing in Las Vegas," and much of his gonzo journalism, are intoxicated with slang, acid talk and a preoccupation with the self.
- Tolstoy, Melville, Hugo, Joyce, Margaret Mitchell, Norman Mailer, Ayn Rand and Arthur Schlesinger Jr. rejected injunctions about brevity, and wrote lengthy, memorable classics.
- James Joyce's "Ulysses" ran to more than 250,000 words. Its 25,000-word final episode provides just a few pauses and one comma.
- Gertrude Stein quipped that "punctuation is necessary only for the feeble-minded." And Cormac McCarthy added, "I mean, if you write properly, you shouldn't have to punctuate."
- Yet Jane Austen's novels, some of the most widely admired in the English language, are full of commas, semicolons, dashes, exclamation marks — on every page.

Good writers, especially fiction writers, enjoy inventing their own rules. Twain did this with distinctive colloquial dialogue. Faulkner made long sentences sing and run-on paragraphs dance.

Raymond Carver triumphed with lean prose. Don DeLillo, in his prize-winning "White Noise," likes verbless sentences. Joyce, in "Finnegans Wake," delights in inventing words, including a 97-letter doozy of a word on page 1.

Ernest Hemingway again merits a note here. Right out of high school, he served a stint as a journalist and was instructed, as is common in that craft, to use short words, short sentences, short paragraphs. Also — keep it positive.

Hemingway carried this over to his fiction writing and worked hard to perfect a lean, spare, no frills, no-clutter style. Thus, we get classic Hemingway sentences such as "It had been bad." and "It was quiet, hot and dirty." He also liked to use "and" in place of commas.

He had his quirks and one was his more debatable fondness for using *very*. Thus he writes sentences such as "It kills the very good and the very gentle and the very brave impartially."

His semi-autobiographical "A Farewell to Arms" (1929) contains hundreds of "*verys*". On one page you read "very nice," "very fine" and "very glad." A few pages later you read, "very tired," "very low" and "very delicate." He gives us five in this paragraph: "The hotel was very big and grand and empty but the food was good, the wine was very pleasant and finally the wine made us all feel very well. Catherine had no need to feel any better. She was very happy. Ferguson became quite cheerful. I felt very well myself."

Hemingway declares someone is "very dead." And at one point our Nobel Prize winner exudes, "I hope you will be very fortunate and very happy and very, very healthy."

The original Hollywood film of this novel, starring Gary Cooper and Helen Hayes, eliminates just about all of Hemingway's "*very*s." Hemingway didn't like the film, yet for other reasons, not the deleted "*very*s."

Here is advice on using "very" --borrowed from a contributing editor to the "Oxford American Writer's Thesaurus," it is as entertaining as it is instructive:

Early on we are taught to be leery of *very* and similar intensives *(exceptionally, especially)*. Indeed, if writers had to do without one of the eight parts of speech, the adverbs would probably be least missed. Yet *very* is among the few words that gains in effectiveness when repeated. *There was definitely something moving around the darkened room. Frightened, Mildred turned the doorknob very, very quietly.* The doubling of *very* slows the sentence down, and conveys a more palpable sense of Mildred's trepidation. Nevertheless, be very, very cautious about using this common adverb, and do so only after thinking twice.[37]

Everyone is entitled to their own tastes. And since everyone else's style is already taken, you're on your own. Be yourself. Find your own voice and style.

More Usage Suggestions

Be careful not to use *feel* when you mean *believe, consider, think.*

Check out how you use the words *but* and *yet. But* cancels what you have just said. *Yet* is used when you are merely adding to what you have said or want a softer reversal than *but. Yet* can mean *nevertheless*, too. "The candidate thought he was going to win, *but* the campaign was now over" (implies he did not win). "The candidate thought he was going to win, yet he had some worries about an issue" (implies he wasn't sure he would win).

Be aware of the difference between *that* and *which. That* defines, which informs. *That* restricts the meaning of a noun and makes it more specific. *Which* adds further information about the subject. The word *that* is more conversational and less formal than the word *which* and many writers prefer using *that* for readability. The traditional rule is that if commas can be inserted around the clause, use *which.*

We use *that* more than *which* while speaking. Crisp writing skips both of them, especially *whiches.* You'll be surprised how often you can either delete them or rewrite sentences not needing them. My vote, for example, is for writing: "She said it's expensive" rather than "She said that it was expensive."

Be careful using *this*. A pronoun refers to a just previous noun, but some writers use *this* to refer to everything they have just said, as in "*This* explains why Donald Trump lost the election." Such usage confuses rather than clarifies.

Even the word *the* can be eliminated in many instances. "When we hear and read it, 'the' doesn't register. Its prevalence numbs us; we're deaf and blind to its ubiquity."[38] Although "the" is sometimes essential, *it* is often superfluous and can often be deleted. Try it.

Use gender-inclusive language. Executives aren't all men, nor are all of those who fish or put out fires. Instead of *fireman*, use *firefighter*. Instead of *congressman*, try *representative*. Use plural forms to avoid sexist language. Instead of "A president will use his veto power," try "Presidents use their veto power." *Human being, humankind, person* and *chair* are substitutes for *man, mankind* and *chairman*.

The pronoun *they* is used to refer to a single person who chooses not to be identified as either female or male.

New Challenges

New words and phrases emerge in every generation: blogosphere, holacracy, block chain, gig-economy, cyberthugs, crowdfunding, cryptocurrency, red states, blue states, purple states, unfriended, flyover states, keto-diets, gaslighting, greenlighting, greenwashing, green premiums, glamping, staycations, voluntourism, data mining, ethereum, brain hacking, ride-hailing, social distancing, psychographics, Big Data, Deep State, Alexa, driverless vehicles, ensorcellment, phishing, homey, meh, nootropics, microfluidics, angel investor, tablet-time, bots, toggle, microtargeting, selfie-stick, karmically, dongles, memes, k-pop, punk'd, locked in, pop-up stores, emojis, alternative facts, truth decay, pressers and punditocracy.

Be aware that many new words have double meanings in social media, for example: *like*/like, *hit*/hit, *cloud*/cloud, *chrome*/chrome, *spam*/spam, *fix*/fix, *fleece*/fleece, *hookup*/hookup, *match*/match, *cookies*/cookies, *bread*/bread, *cool*/cool. *draft*/draft, *wasted*/wasted, *angel*/angel, *stud*/stud, *chill*/chill, *snowflake*/snowflake, *chick*/chick, *unicorn*/unicorn, and *woke, poke, pawn, money, mouse, rock, vintage, culture.*

When and how to best use abbreviations? It is hard enough to remember how to abbreviate the names of states. Yet it is amazing how many people, groups and organizations we do recognize by their initials. Here's a quick acronym test: ABC, CBS, PBS, NBC, NPR, NFT, SPAC, MSNBC, NBA, NFL, YMCA, NRA, NASA, IRS, NSF, POW, MIA, CIA, CYA, UCLA, MTA, JFK, LBJ, AOC, EU, EV, AI, ETF, NDA, PTSD, ISIS, OMG, UPS, BMW, AWD, CDC, DOD, LGBTQ, VISA, NATO, FANG, DMZ, CBD, THC, LSD, MACA, LOL, GOAT, etc. ... If you understood 20 or more, you pass.

The Associated Press recommends spelling out dates and addresses when, for example, you write, "I was born in November 1970" and "I live on Main Street." But abbreviate when giving more specific information: "I was born on Nov. 17, 1970" and "I live at 123 Main St."

Every sport develops its own vocabulary. American baseball provides *home run, home plate, fast ball, curve ball, sinker, change-up, grand slam, brush-ball, dugout, foul ball, Texas-leaguer, walk-off home run* and countless more. Tennis gives us *deuce, lob, love, overhead smash, ace* and *fault.* Football gives us *red zones, sacks* and *take it to the house.* Golf gives us *teeing-up.* A *birdie* refers to a golfer who succeeds in getting the ball to the hole one stroke below the official par for that hole. *Mulligan* is a golf term for a "do-over" or "correction shot" when one's first shot has gone astray. These sports terms get adopted as metaphors in everyday conversation. For example, a last-ditch try is a *Hail Mary pass* (from football), a sure outcome is a *slam-dunk*, a *layup* is an easy shot close to the basket (from basketball) and a muscular free-for-all is a *scrum* (from rugby). A *gamer* or *baller* is a player who is *in the zone,* or *locked in* or *dialed in.* Yet beware of clichés, such as "he lost his fast ball" or "she's out in left field." Sports clichés can be among the worst.

The worlds of finance, music and the internet also have their own specialized vocabularies. Gretchen McCulloch's "Because Internet: Understanding the New Rules of Language" explains the new "internetty" rules and style. Texting, for example, has minimal punctuation and rarely uses complete sentences. Using all caps means one is SHOUTING; and emoticons or memes convey feelings or judgments. LOL or lol means laughing out loud.

McCulloch examines how the internet encourages a new creativity as well as more slang. She is optimistic and ☺ about most of these new developments and chides grumpy grammarians who are alarmed at the remixing and cleverness of internet culture.[39]

Additional Style Suggestions

I like reading forcefully argued essays. Yet, like most people, I'm put off by overstatement. Understated writing usually works better. Effective writers learn the right balance for their audience.

An exclamation mark is a period that "blew its top." Newspaper editors call them "screamers." Use them sparingly. Avoid unnecessary underlining, italicizing and boldfacing for the same reason. A well-constructed sentence creates its own emphasis.

Parentheses explain or provide incidental information. But they can jar the reader, interrupting the sentence flow with some additional, secondary information. Most sentences can be rewritten to avoid their use.

The same is true for hyphens and dashes. A hyphen (a short dash) is used for compound words, as in "long-needed legislation." Using a hyphen can also avoid ambiguity, for example: "Did you mean *old movie-buff* or *old-movie buff?*" Here are a few hyphenated regulars: well-known, self-reliant, half-baked and cross-country.

A dash, or "en dash" (the length of two hyphens), makes for informal dialogue, and amplifies or shifts a point of view. Novelists use dashes to make a character's dialogue or thoughts appear spontaneous. The poet Emily Dickinson was a dasher.

The dash, used correctly, creates a dramatic pause to introduce an idea or expression meriting emphasis.

Yet expository writers limit their use of dashes to avoid choppiness. Language maven William Safire satirizes the dramatic writer's penchant for the dash and similar punctuation novelties: "Writers of drama must write speech, not writing, because real people do not speak writing. Hence we have pauses, delays — you get my drift? — half-stops, restarts, stammering, and exclamatory grunts (ugh!) and drifting off into pre-dot-com ellipses. ... To put this speech in written form — that is, to transcribe it — we have seen the powerful punch —pow! Right in the kisser — of illustrative punctuation."[40]

You can also use a longer dash, called an "em dash," the length of 2½ hyphens. On my old MacBook Pro, I hit "alt," then minus sign twice. On PCs, hit control, alt and the hyphen on your keypad, on the right side of your keyboard.

Some editors frown on "em dashes." Others are OK with it, if it is used sparingly. The "em dash is," writes defender Kate Mooney, "emphatic, agile and still largely undefined. Sometimes it indicates an afterthought. Other times, it's a fist pump. You might call it the bad boy or cool girl of punctuation. A freewheeling scofflaw."[41] The em-dash helps to set off a clause or word, adding emphasis. For example: "She was opposed to two things — dogma and authoritarianism.

Finally, since we are talking about dashes, there is the squishy, slightly drunken dash called a "tilde" (~). In scientific writing, the tilde indicates *approximately*. It can be used as a shorthand way to indicate approximate dates, or data points.

Although parentheses, hyphens and dashes may make it easier to explain what you mean, beware of overusing them. Each use makes its own little stop in the flow of reading. When in doubt about using them, you can consult "The Chicago Manual of Style" or the "Modern Language Association Handbook for Writers of Research Papers."

A comma indicates a natural pause in a sentence, a place where one adjective or phrase has ended and another begins. "The comma was invented to help readers. Without it, sentence parts can collide with one another unexpectedly, causing misreadings."[42] Too many commas, however, make a sentence confusing, with too many stops and starts to retain the overall meaning. *"Comma sense"* is knowing how and when to use commas. The best way to learn how to use them is to pay attention to good writers and "reverse-engineer" their sentences.

A colon (:) is used to present an explanation or a list, or introduce a quotation. A colon means *"thus"* with an explanation to follow. For example, "The legislator brought home the bacon: a bridge, a new post office and a new veteran's hospital."

A semicolon (;) connects two independent clauses, when each clause is a complete sentence in itself and the two sentences are strongly related in meaning. Writers and editors debate how to use semicolons. Cecelia Watson, in a short history, "Semicolon," says it dates back to at least 1494 in Venice. "It was meant" she writes, "to signify a pause of length somewhere between that of a comma and that of the colon, and its heritage was reflected in its form, which combines half of each of those marks."[43]

George Orwell and Kurt Vonnegut dissed semicolons as pretentious. Norman Mailer would rewrite a whole page to avoid using a semicolon. And this wry warning is attributed to Mark Twain, among others: "Don't use semicolons. ... All they do is show you've been to college."

Others contend semicolons can clarify and enhance readability. The acclaimed Herman Melville used thousands of semicolons. And Martin Luther King, Jr.'s "Letter from Birmingham City Jail" is an example of the effective use of semicolons.

Use punctuation carefully. To paraphrase "The Chicago Manual of Style," punctuation should be used in service of clarity, readability and a compelling style.

Commas and periods go inside quote marks, and colons and semicolons go after quote marks. Question marks and exclamation marks depend on the context.

If the punctuation mark is part of the quote or title, it goes inside the quote marks. For instance: "Have you seen 'Little Women'?" and "I really loved 'Who Framed Roger Rabbit?'!"

If the passage after a colon is a complete sentence, it should be capitalized.

Vary the length of your sentences and paragraphs, and vary how you begin your sentences. Nothing bores a reader more than a string of paragraphs starting with "*Harry Truman said...*" "*Harry Truman declared…"* or *"As Harry Truman noted…"* Watch out for beginning every paragraph with *"There is…" "It seems that there were…,"* etc. Instead, keep your audience awake. Use variety and counterpoint, occasional short sentences, and one- or two-sentence paragraphs. Keep your readers engaged, not only with the ideas you are talking about, but also with their own act of reading.

Tables and Numbers

Use tables only when necessary. Sometimes they are. I like tables and visual displays of data. Yet readers have a tendency to skip past them, viewing them as intrusions or merely as evidence for a point the author makes in the prose. Try summarizing the contents of a table in prose and showing it in an eye-catching visual (as in USA Today or CNBC displays), so it can be grasped at a glance.

As a rule, tables or figures should stand on their own. They should be understandable to the reader who has not yet read the narrative. The meaning of numbers should be clear. Yet tables and graphs shouldn't be relied on to make a point not already made in the text; they should only amplify a point.

A table can help summarize data or highlight particular things to clarify research findings for the reader. "Including a table in a paper does not," however, "relieve you of the obligation to describe specifically what is in that table," writes Raymond Wolfinger. "You should not solve the problem of data description by instructing readers to look at Table 2 if they want to know what you found."[44]

Write out numbers from one to nine, round numbers and when a number begins a sentence. Thus, as examples, there are about 1,440 words in the Declaration of Independence, 10 court rulings, eight vetoes, 65 legislative measures. Spell out "percent" except in tables. Spell out ordinal numbers, such as "the twenty-first century," or "the top one percent. "Use numerals for dates, e.g., *Jan. 20, 2024,* and for legislative sessions, e.g., *110th Congress.* Note, however, "The Chicago Manual of Style" recommends writers should spell out whole numbers from zero to one hundred.

Make sure your numbers add up correctly in any table or chart. Errors, especially in percentages, easily creep into reports.

Quotations and Citations

Use quotations selectively. Few observations are truly original. The use of too many quotations conceals from the reader what you have learned, what you know and what you think. Quotations interrupt flow just as readily as using too many tables, parentheses or foreign phrases. Include long quotations only when the exact wording is crucial to your argument.

After you have read widely on a topic, you develop a sense of what is common knowledge. Dictionary definitions, the date of Picasso's death, Ronald Reagan's career in Hollywood or Donald Trump's career as a developer and television host don't need to be cited or quoted from other sources. Paraphrase agreed-on definitions and common knowledge. If you know something, you can probably say it just as well as someone else did, and adapt the information to suit your purposes. You should shorten it as well. You can still give proper credit to the author who inspired your thoughts. Reserve quotations for material that is colorful, opinionated or distinctive. Also, quotations should merely support your argument rather than make a point for you.

If you use a quotation that runs five or six lines in your typescript, set it off as a block quotation. Indent it half an inch from the left margin of the text and double-space it. I prefer the old way of single-spacing quotations, but new writing handbooks often mandate double-spacing. Indented blocked quotations don't have quotation marks. Keep in mind, however, that most of us let our eyes dance past block quotations. Shortening them so that they're integrated into the text increases reader attention.

Another device to keep your reader with you is to identify the author in the middle of a quotation rather than in the more traditional beginning or ending tag. Try putting a quotation this way: "I suppose I have written *the fact that* a thousand times in the heat of composition, revised it out maybe five hundred times in the cool aftermath," writes E.B. White. "To be batting only .500 this late in the season, to fail half the time to connect with this fast pitch, saddens me, for it seems a betrayal of [my mentor] who showed me how to swing at it and made the swinging seem worthwhile."[45]

Keep notes or a journal of quotations you might decide to use in your writing later on. Take down the author's words accurately, and record the source in full. Errors occur in quotations and citations, and retracing your steps to correct them is both time-consuming and frustrating at later stages in your work.

To shorten a quotation a writer can use the ellipsis notation (…). *Ellipsis*, a Greek word, means leaving out. Thus you can leave out an unneeded phrase in a sentence, as in *"The president … reiterated his support for the constitutional amendment,"* so long as what remains is grammatical. When omitting a full sentence, end the previous sentence with a period, then space once before adding the ellipsis.

Give credit to the appropriate sources for direct quotations and the distinctive ideas you paraphrase from others. The more you write, however, the more you will want to skip verbose quotes you may have cited when you were less well-read. Learn to be selective: "The art of handling quotes comes down to knowing when to quote, when to paraphrase, when to forget the whole thing."[46]

Footnotes are required tools for manuscripts. They're not needed for short stories, texting or newspaper opinion essays. Footnote information you have learned from a book, article, newspaper or interview if it is something others would not know without access to that source. Footnote material can encourage readers to explore ideas or related topics in greater detail elsewhere.

Plagiarism is copying part or all of another's work without citing the source. It also refers to using someone's phrasing and ideas without proper credit. Plagiarism is cheating. "Your research paper is a collaboration between you and your sources," writes Diana Hacker. "To be fair and ethical, you must acknowledge your debt to the writers of those sources."[47]

Whenever you use another writer's exact words, you must enclose words or sentences in quotation marks. Changing one or two words doesn't make it your sentence.

Leads and Conclusions

Be creative in choosing an apt and, if possible, intriguing title. An effective title telegraphs your theme and arouses interest.

First impressions matter. First sentences are important. A stylish lead signals your thesis and can hook readers with calculated teasers. Journalists sometimes use the word "lede" for lead. Leads must entice the reader to read into and complete the story. Effective leads are often short, snappy and savvy. As readers look at your title and leading sentences, they ask: What's the big idea? Where is this writer going? What's in it for me?

Reporters devote considerable energy to making "the top of the story" accurate and arresting. Why? Readers don't get beyond the first two paragraphs of most stories in newspapers and magazines. If a writer grabs your attention up front, they have a chance to hold your interest for the duration.

> The lead must capture the reader immediately and force him to keep reading. It must cajole him with freshness or novelty or paradox, or with humor, or with surprise, or with an

unusual idea, or an interesting fact, or a question. Anything will do as long as it nudges his curiosity and tugs at his sleeve.

Next the lead must do some real work. It must provide a few hard details that tell the reader why the piece was written and why he ought to read it. But don't dwell on the reason. Coax the reader a little more; keep him inquisitive.[48]

Although news writing is different from college essays, corporate reports or public policy papers, introductions in every form of writing are important. Students have the good fortune — although some might quibble at this description — those professors are paid to read student papers from start to finish even if the leads aren't arresting, and despite, in too many instances, their paper being totally lame. Yet duty doesn't guarantee interest. Students, like everyone else, should make the best possible case for the significance of their essays at the outset.

Yet don't let your lead mislead. "A lead is good," writes John McPhee, "not because it dances, fires cannons, or whistles like a train, but because it is absolute to what follows."[49]

Good leads often can't be written until an essay is finished. Try writing several leads after you've finished your first draft. Don't be too quick to settle on the first. Let leads emerge.

For long papers — more than 20 pages — subheads are helpful in indicating transitions to new material or new sections. Subheads can add to a paper's readability and, cleverly used, can save words. Yet, as most college writing as well as professional assignments are five to 15 pages and focus on a few major points, subheadings and section breaks may be unnecessary. Beware of using subheads as a crutch to avoid writing transitions between different ideas.

Conclusions should flow from the rest of the paper. They should tie ideas together, not simply restate what already has been said. Nor should they introduce new topics or information. The best conclusions explore the significance of the idea in the essay, sometime by making recommendations. They can open up new conversations about other possibilities, alternative lines of inquiry.

Format and Presentation

Find out if your intended reader (professor, supervisor, board of directors, legislative committee, editors, et al.) has specific requirements about the format of your paper. If there are no specific requirements, it is a good idea to type double-spaced, font 12 or14 point, use margins of one inch, staple in upper left corner, put your name and date in upper right corner, and skip a title page or binder.

Here are common sense suggestions. Most people already know them, yet what you know and what you do are not necessarily the same.

Proofread your paper two or three times before submitting it. Even then, you'll spot an occasional typo or error just as you are submitting it. What to do? Correct the error by hand, and be sure to correct your saved computer copy. Always save and date each draft of your essay in appropriate document file (*draft 1*, *draft 2*, etc.).

On occasion, you may want to append at the end of your essay a brief *Author's Note* or *Afterword*. This is not a place for excuses or apologies, but rather a place to indicate your feelings about the topic or controversy, or how your views changed as you did the research and writing. It might be a place, too, to mention some unusual circumstance under which you wrote. Or perhaps you want to note how joyous or exacting the assignment became. Once again, some teachers, supervisors and editors may object to this practice. You'll have to judge whether the context warrants an *Author's Note,* an *Afterword* or, perhaps, an *Epilogue.*

Writer's Block

Daunted by a writing assignment? You're not alone. John Steinbeck said he suffered from "the fear of putting words down for the first time." And Gabriel Garcia Marquez quipped that, "all my life, I've been frightened at the moment I sat down to write."

"Like climbing a mountain, writing a book is exciting at the beginning, exhilarating at the end, but tedious, frustrating, and hair-raising in between," writes Ralph Keyes.[50]

How does a writer overcome fear and get "in the zone," put anxieties aside and encourage original ideas to flow? Keyes suggests the following "courage boosters":[51]

- Read about successful writers and learn how they dealt with their fears and anxieties.
- Talk to other writers: join a writers' group, attend a conference or take a writing course.
- Try to convert fear into excitement: Learn how to deal with your internal critic and get to know yourself well

enough not to be terrified by what escapes from within onto the page.

Changing your habits or rituals may also help. If you usually write at night, experiment with writing in the morning. If you write on a computer, try writing on a legal pad, or vice versa. Vary your exercise patterns. A swim, jog, yoga workout, meditation session or deep-breathing routine may help.

Another suggestion for dealing with writer's block is to try different venues. J.K. Rowling wrote her early "Harry Potter" novels in coffee houses. Writers have written novels on their commuter trains and in backyard sheds. A few political prisoners have written memoirs on toilet paper. Other writers write best in a favorite room. Some schedule their writing at the same time and in the same room each day. Some write from dawn to noon. One friend of mine writes from 8 p.m. to 4 a.m. on a regular basis. Former President Barack Obama says he does his best writing between 10 p.m. and 2 a.m. Some dictate portions of their writing.

Beethoven took long walks in the countryside, making notes about musical ideas in a notebook he carried with him. Try his method: Take a prepared list of a dozen questions with you and, as you walk, jot down ideas next to these questions. You may be surprised to find how much material you have when you return to your computer.

To ease writer's block, set measurable productivity goals and then reward yourself on achieving them. Remember the maxim: "The perfect is the enemy of the good."

Most writing problems are human problems. Courage and honesty, curiosity and fearlessness, discipline and persistence are key. Nothing is as important as the urge to share a story, to explore the truth, to get people to understand one another.

Writing as a Performing Art

Writing is a craft. It is also a performance. Unlike music or drama or sports, no conductor or director or coach leads a reader through writing. Instead, it is you, the writer, directly communicating one-to-one with your reader. Your word selections, the pace and pitch of your sentences, and your punctuation marks tell the reader how to read. Your ideas — and how you present them — provoke the reader to think or feel or imagine. Writing is a performance in that you are giving, sharing or demonstrating, and your audience — the reader — participates in this performance through their reading, responding and applauding, or maybe groaning.

Part of what the reader does, in the act of reading, is to ask: Does this make sense? Do I believe the writer? Am I persuaded? What happens next? Is this fun to read? Does this writing have character — and do I like the voice of this writer? Is the evidence convincing? Why should I care?

For an effective "performance," a writer must find voice, purpose and inner drive. "What I have most wanted to do throughout the past ten years is to make political writing into an art," writes George Orwell.

"Looking back," he adds, "I see that it is invariably where I lacked a political purpose that I wrote lifeless books and was betrayed into purple passages, sentences without meaning, decorative adjectives and humbug generally."[52] To write honestly, with power, voice and courage, you first have to make an appointment with yourself, unleash your curiosity, listen, observe and come to terms with your values. Writers typically write from the "inside out" rather than the "outside in."

The best advice, if you want to become an effective writer, is to read great books, as many as possible. Read the Greek classics, the Old and New Testaments, the sonnets and plays of Shakespeare, the novels of Tolstoy, Victor Hugo and George Orwell. Read well-written, well-edited magazines, such as The New Yorker, The Economist, Science, Nature, The Atlantic and The New York Review of Books. Discover well-researched, well-organized podcasts. Keep a journal with your own comments on fine writing and what you like and dislike. Start a collection of words you like. Develop your own lists of pet peeve, weasel, trans-fat or hedging words. Heighten your awareness about the power of words.

Writing As A Performing Art

Hemingway said the way a young writer learns the craft is just to go away and write. Yet it helps to have mentors. Hemingway himself grew up on a steady diet of Jack London, Mark Twain and similar storytellers. And he was trained by newspaper editors in Kansas and Toronto. After World War I, he went to Paris and enjoyed "tutorial sessions" with Gertrude Stein and Sherwood Anderson.

You can "adopt" gifted writers as your mentors. Read and reread your favorite writers, columnists and social scientists. If you have no favorites, try Jefferson, Lincoln, Twain, Churchill, Steinbeck, Hemingway, Fitzgerald, Raymond Carver, Nadine Gordimer, Anthony Lewis, Lewis Thomas, Calvin Trillin, Anna Quindlen and Tim O'Brien. Read the Latin writers Carlos Fuentes, Isabel Allende, Gabriel Garcia Marquez and Manuel Puig. Read their earlier works.

Discover why these writers are good: How do they structure the progression of ideas or events? How do they capture your attention? How do they persuade you of a point of view? How do they treat evidence? When do they simplify? What passages speak most clearly to you, and why?

Novice writers may profit from examining the paradoxes of leadership and life. You can learn, too, from Zen Buddhist poems, verses and koans. Koans are puzzles, paradoxical riddles or questions used in meditation. They help some to unravel, or at least ponder, the dialectics of the human condition. "What is the sound of one hand clapping?" and "How high is no?" are examples. Another koan:

> *If you understand,*
> *things are just as they are;*
> *If you do not understand,*
> *things are just as they are.*[53]

To write well, you have to be willing to revise extensively. "I began to write seriously when I had taught myself the discipline necessary to achieve what I wanted," observes novelist Bernard Malamud. "When I touched that time, my words announced themselves to me." Revision, he notes, became not only essential but also one of the exquisite pleasures of writing. He would write everything three times: once to understand it, the second time to improve the prose, "and a third time to say what it still must say."[54]

Learn from feedback, both critical and positive. A later detached reading of what you have written will be as revealing as it is rewarding. Gaps between what you wrote and what you meant become apparent. Awkward transitions or unnecessary apologies jump out at you. Doubleheaders, redundancies, zombies, clichés, solecisms and "twinkies" pop up. Revise, revise.

Set high expectations for your project, yet remember that perfectionism undermines playfulness, creativity and the liberating process of writing. "Perfectionism is the voice of the oppressor. ... It will keep you cramped and insane your whole life," writes Anne Lamott.[55] Messiness and improvisation are the writer's friends.

Pace yourself on specific writing assignments. Too much time devoted to research often leaves too little for stylish writing. An executive friend has a helpful 70 percent rule: Though having all the information would be perfect, having two-thirds or so of the available information usually results in making an appropriate decision. Nutritionists similarly talk of an 80 or 90 percent rule: If you eat your fruit and veggies most of the time, you can indulge occasionally in dark chocolate or a glass of wine.

Few scholars can do all the experiments, read all the literature and obtain all the data, interviews and evidence they'd like to have before making judgments. Three cheers for rigorous, controlled experiments. They are, of course, necessary for medical and related scientific research work. Yet executives or writers who wait for 100 percent assurances may be waiting long after it has been worth the effort. The bus headed for "Perfection" rarely, if ever, comes to our local stop. Beware the "ready, aim, aim" syndrome. Writers must be willing to make decisions, come to judgments and commit.

If you have important ideas to share, writing badly is still better than not writing at all.[56] Precise grammar and efficiency have their virtues, yet creativity and innovation are intrinsically messy. Many of us are prisoners of grumpy grammarians who railed against our sloppy sentences and seemed to care too little about what we were trying to say — the tyranny of form over substance. What's the use of elegant writing that's allergic to any substance? You don't want to be the person who can speak fluently in six languages, yet has nothing to say in any of them.

"Timing is everything" says an aphorism. And we're told that "the early bird gets the worm." Yet writers need to put this bromide in context. For it is typically the second and not the first mouse that gets the cheese. Moreover, it might not be the first, or even the second, storyteller who writes the best version of a tale. Shakespeare famously retold and reworked many of his plays from material borrowed from the Greek writer Plutarch and others. We honor the English bard for his ingenious retelling.

Writing matters. But what matters even more is the power of ideas. Just as leaders define, defend and promote important mutually shared values, writers help define and clarify critical choices. Writing is a grand opportunity to tell your story, tell the truth, advocate beliefs, share creative ideas and celebrate our capacity for compassion, gallantry, humanity and love. And to "take it to the house."

Writers benefit from deadlines and learn to embrace the "letting go" process. There comes a point — for writers, artists and composers — where you can make it different, yet probably not better. Put it out there and move on to your next project.

Great writers help shape their times. Harriet Beecher Stowe led the way to emancipation. Churchill's influence came from his ability to inspire by both spoken and written word. Martin Luther

King, Jr.'s "Letter from Birmingham City Jail" and "I Have a Dream" speech galvanized the U.S. civil rights movement in the early 1960s. Rachel Carson's "Silent Spring" and Betty Friedan's "The Feminine Mystique" helped launch impressive movements. The writings of Karl Marx and Milton Friedman redefined economic debates. Inspirational writers from Thomas Paine and Henry David Thoreau to Elie Wiesel have transformed people's lives, just as the writings of Peter Drucker and James MacGregor Burns clarified our understanding of leadership. The power of the pen and word processor are different from the power of the sword yet should never be underestimated.

Writers write to record the truth of their time and to heighten the possibilities for freedom and justice, peace and prosperity. They write to confront hypocrisy, injustice, myth and conventional wisdom. They write to help us understand ourselves, one another and our universe.

Here is my parting blessing:

> *May you find the right words*
> *On a cool morning, and*
> *A full and*
> *Inspiring moon on a dark night*
> *May the muse of curiosity and*
> *Imagination offer*
> *Enriching perspective, and*
> *May you have the wind at your back*
> *and a downhill trail*
> *As you write*
> > *Fearlessly,*
> > > *Frequently, and*
> > > *Joyously....*

Footnotes

1. William Zinsser, "On Writing Well: The Classic Guide to Writing Nonfiction." (Harper Perennial, 2006), p. 96.

2. Ibid., p. 297.

3. For more on this, see Thomas E. Cronin, "Imagining a Great Republic: Political Novels and the Idea of America." (Lanham, Md: Rowman & Littlefield, 2018).

4. Kurt Vonnegut, "How to Write with Style," Newsweek on Campus, April 1987, pp. 54-55.

5. Pico Iyer, "In Praise of the Humble Comma," Time, June 13, 1988, p. 80.

6. Ernest Hemingway, excerpts from letters to friends, in Larry W. Phillips, ed., "Ernest Hemingway on Writing." (New York: Scribner's, 1984), p. 77. And from an interview, in George Plimpton, ed., "Writers at Work," (New York: Viking, 1965), p. 222.

7. Aleksandr Solzhenitsyn, Nobel Prize address, 1970, in John Hersey, "The Writer's Craft." (New York: Knopf, 1974), pp. 148 and 151.

8. Gerald Graff and Cathy Birkenstein, "They Say/I Say." (New York: W.W. Norton, 2006), p. 3.

9. David Pion-Berlin, *Reflections on Writing a Dissertation*, in "PS: Political Science and Politics." (Winter 1986), p. 64.

10. E.L. Doctorow, quoted in Travis Elborough and Helen Gordon, "Being a Writer." (London: Quarto, 2017), p. 68.

11. For more on the role of creative destruction in America, see Alan Greenspan and Adrian Wooldridge, "Capitalism in America: A History." (New York: Penguin, 2018).

12. For more on this topic, see Thomas S. Kuhn, "The Structure of Scientific Revolutions," 2nd ed. (Chicago: University of Chicago Press, 1970). Follow the lead of Columbus, Galileo and Darwin. See also Safi Bahcall, "Loonshots: How to Nurture the Crazy Ideas that Win Wars, Cure Diseases, and Transform Industries." (New York: St. Martin's Press, 2019).

13. Somerset Maugham, quoted in James Charlton and Lisbeth Mark, "The Writer's Home Companion." (New York: Franklin Watts, 1987), p. 77. See also George Orwell, "Politics and the English Language," originally written in 1946; reprinted in George Orwell, "The Orwell Reader." (New York: Harcourt, Brace, 1956), pp. 355-66.

14. Kate L. Turabian, "Student's Guide for Writing College Papers," 3rd ed. (Chicago: University of Chicago Press, 1976), p. 40.

15. Wendy R. Leibowitz, *Technology Transforms Writing and the Teaching of Writing*, "Chronicle of Higher Education." Nov. 26, 1999, p. 67.

16. Sylvan Barnet, "A Short Guide to Writing about Art," 2nd ed. (Boston: Little, Brown, 1985), p. 74.

17. Peter Elbow, "Writing with Power: Techniques for Mastering the Writing Process." (New York: Oxford University Press, 1981), p. 299.

18. Trish Hall, "Writing to Persuade." (New York: Liveright, 2019), p. 136. My listing of her suggestions is adapted from throughout her book.

19. Peter Elbow, "Writing with Power." p. 123.

20. Stanley Kunitz, in answer to a student's question in a poetry class at Whitman College, Nov. 5, 1997. See also his *Speaking of Poetry* in his "Passing Through: The Later Poems." (New York: Norton, 1995), p. 11.

21. Anne Lamott, "Bird by Bird: Some Instructions on Writing and Life." (New York: Anchor Books, 1995), pp. 25-26.

22. Jacques Barzun, *Lincoln the Writer,* in his "On Writing, Editing and Publishing," 2nd ed. (Chicago: University of Chicago Press, 1986), p. 81.

23. James J. Kilpatrick, "The Writer's Art." (Kansas City: Andrews, McMeel and Parker, 1984), p. 54.

24. William Strunk, Jr., and E.B. White, "The Elements of Style," 3rd ed. (New York: Athenaeum, 1965), p. 140.

25. John Kenneth Galbraith, "A Life in Our Times: Memoirs." (Boston: Houghton Mifflin, 1981), pp. 535-6.

26. Trish Hall, "Writing to Persuade." (New York: Liveright, 2019), p. 19, p. 147.

27. Rene J. Cappon, "The Word: An Associated Press Guide to Good News Writing." (New York: Associated Press, 1982), p. 22.

28. Theodore M. Bernstein, "The Careful Writer: A Modern Guide to Usage." (New Athenaeum, 1965), p. 140.

29. Zinsser, "On Writing Well." p. 71.

30. Steven Pinker, "The Sense of Style." (New York: Viking, 2014) p. 43 and p. 44.

31. These suggestions come from Joseph M. Williams, "Style," 2nd ed. (Glenview, Ill: Scott, Foresman and Co., 1985), p. 88.

32. Cappon, "The Word." p. 110.

33. Culled from a longer list in "The Oxford American Writer's Thesaurus." (New York: Oxford University Press, 2004, pp. 1,085-1,087), and from Harold Evans, "Do I Make Myself Clear?" (New York: Little, Brown, 2017), pp. 160. And elsewhere …

34. See Diana Hacker, "A Pocket Style Manual," 4th ed. (Boston: Bedford/St. Martin's, 2004), pp. 19-20, and Theodore M. Bernstein, "The Careful Reader." (New York: Athenaeum, 1965), pp. 1,003-5.

35. Helen Sword, "Stylish Academic Writing." (Cambridge: Harvard University Press, 2012), p. 61. Also see Sword's "The Writer's Diet." (Chicago: University of Chicago Press, 2016), p. 21.

36. Mary Norris, "Between You and Me: Confessions of a Comma Queen." (New York: Norton, 2015), p. 168. See also Theodore M. Bernstein, "Miss Thistlebottom's Hobgoblins." (New York: Farrar, Straus and Giroux, 1971), pp. 183-184.

37. Michael Dirda, contributing editor, "The Oxford American Writer's Thesaurus," (Oxford University Press, 2004), p. 989.

38. Jim Triggs, "To 'the' or Not to 'the'?", Wall Street Journal, June 5, 2013, p. A11.

39. Gretchen McCulloch, "Because Internet: Understanding the New Rules of Language." (New York: Riverhead Books, 2019).

40. William Safire, "Dash It All." New York Times Magazine, May 28, 2000, p. 19.

41. Kate Mooney, "A Divisive Punctuation Mark Stands Alone." The New York Times, Aug. 15, 2019, p. D5.

42. Hacker, "A Pocket Style Manual," 4th ed., p. 17. See also the comma usage suggestions in Mary Norris, "Between You & Me," Chapter 1. "Parentheses," Norris writes, "often act like giant commas, and commas like tiny parentheses," p. 103.

43. Cecilia Watson, "Semicolon: The Past, Present, and Future of a Misunderstood Mark." (New York: Ecco, 2019), p. 13.

44. Raymond E. Wolfinger, "Tips for Writing Papers," PS: Political Science and Politics, March 1993, p. 88.

45. E.B. White, Introduction to Strunk and White, "Elements of Style," 3rd ed., p. xiv.

46. Cappon, "The Word." p. 71.

47. Hacker, "A Pocket Style Manual," 4th ed., p. 157. See also Richard A. Posner, "The Little Book of Plagiarism," (New York, Pantheon Books, 2007).

48. Zinsser, "On Writing Well." p. 6. See also Marshall Cook, "How to Write Good Article Leads," Writer Magazine, June 1987, pp. 16-18.

49. John McPhee, "Draft No. 4." (New York: Farrar, Straus and Giroux, 2017), p. 510.

50. Ralph Keyes, "The Courage to Write." (New York: Henry Holt and Co., 1995), p. 190.

51. Ibid, pp. 200-1.

52. George Orwell, "Why I Write," 1946, quoted in Bernard Crick, "George Orwell." (Boston: Atlantic — Little, Brown, 1980), p. xiii.

53. For a popular book on koans, see John Tarrant, "Bring Me the Rhinoceros: And Other Koans that Will Save Your Life." (Boulder: Shambhala, 2008). For more on paradoxes, see Thomas E. Cronin and Michael A. Genovese, "Leadership Matters: Unlocking the Power of Paradoxes" (Boulder, Paradigm, 2012).

54. Bernard Malamud, "Reflections of a Writer," lecture at Bennington College, Oct. 30, 1984, quoted in New York Times Book Review, March 20, 1988, p. 18.

55. Anne Lamott, "Bird by Bird: Some Instructions on Writing and Life." (New York: Anchor, 1995), p. 28.

56. Bruce Ballenger, "The Importance of Writing Badly", Christian Science Monitor, March 28, 1990, p. 16.

Helpful Works on Style and Usage

Associated Press, "The Associated Press Stylebook and Briefing on Media Law," 55th ed. New York: Basic Books, 2020.

Sheridan Baker, "The Practical Stylist." New York: Crowell, 1969.

Sylvan Barnet, "A Short Guide to Writing about Art," 8th ed. Boston: Little, Brown, 2005.

Jacques Barzun, "Simple & Direct: A Rhetoric for Writers." New York: HarperCollins, 2001.

Theodore M. Bernstein, "The Careful Writer: A Modern Guide to Usage." New York: Atheneum, 1965.

Theodore M. Bernstein, "Miss Thistlebottom's Hobgoblins." New York: Farrar, Straus and Giroux, 1971.

Wayne C. Booth, et al., "The Craft of Research." Chicago: University of Chicago Press, 1995.

Ray Bradbury, "Zen in the Art of Writing." Santa Barbara: Capra Press, 1990.

Laura Brown, "The Only Business Writing Book You'll Ever Need." New York: Norton, 2019.

Rene J. Cappon, "The Word: An Associated Press Guide to Good News Writing." New York: Associated Press, 1982.

"The Chicago Manual of Style," 15th ed. Chicago: University of Chicago Press, 2003.

Fredrick Crews, "The Random House Handbook," 3rd ed. New York: Random House, 1980.

Timothy W. Crusius and Carolyn E. Channell, "The Aims of Argument," 6th ed. New York: McGraw Hill, 2008.

Ann Curzan, "The Secret Life of Words: English Words and Their Origins." Chantilly, Virginia: The Teaching Company, 2012.

Benjamin Dreyer, "Dreyer's English." New York: Random House, 2019.

Peter Elbow, "Writing with Power." Oxford: Oxford University Press, 1998.

Peter Elbow, "Writing without Teachers." Oxford University

Rudolf Flesch, "The Art of Readable Writing." New York: Collier, 1949.

Rudolf Flesch and A.H. Lass, "A New Guide to Better Writing." New York: Warner Books, 1983.

Harold Evans, "Do I Make Myself Clear." New York: Little, Brown, 2017.

Bryan A. Garner, "A Dictionary of Modern American Usage." New York: Oxford University Press, 1998.

Joseph Gibald, "MLA Handbook for Writers of Research Papers," 6th ed. New York: Modern Language Association of America, 2003.

Natalie Goldberg, "Writing Down the Bones: Freeing the Writer Within." Boston: Shambhala, 1986.

Karen Elizabeth Gordon, "The Deluxe Transitive Vampire: The Ultimate Handbook of Grammar for the Innocent, the Eager, and the Doomed." New York: Pantheon, 1993.

Gerald Graff and Cathy Birkenstein, "They Say/I Say: The Moves that Matter in Academic Writing." New York: W.W. Norton, 2006.

Diana Hacker, "A Pocket Style Manual." 4th ed. Boston: Bedford/St. Martin's, 2004.

Donald Hall, "Writing Well." Boston: Little, Brown, 1985.

Trish Hall, "Writing to Persuade." New York: Liveright, 2019.

John Hersey, "The Writer's Craft." New York: Knopf, 1974.

Thomas S. Kane. "The New Oxford Guide to Writing." New York: Oxford University Press, 1994.

Ralph Keyes, "The Courage to Write: How Writers Transcend Fear." New York: Henry Holt and Co., 1995.

James J. Kilpatrick, "The Writer's Art." Kansas City: Andrew, McMeel and Parker, 1984.

Stephen King, "On Writing: A Memoir of the Craft." New York: Scribner, 2000.

Anne Lamott, "Bird by Bird: Some Instructions on Writing and Life." New York: Anchor, 1995.

Richard A. Lanham, "Revising Prose," 2nd ed. New York: Macmillan, 1987.

Andrea A. Lunsford, "The Everyday Writer." Boston: Bedford/St. Martin's, 2001.

Andrea A. Lunsford and John J. Ruszkiewicz, "Everything's an Argument," 3rd ed. Boston: Bedford/St. Martin's, 2004.

Gretchen McCulloch, "Because Internet: Understanding the New Rules of Language." New York: Riverhead Books, 2019.

John McPhee, "Draft No. 4: On the Writing Process." New York: Farrar, Straus and Giroux, 2017.

Casey Miller and Kate Smith, "The Handbook of Nonsexist Writing," 2nd ed. New York: Harper & Row, 1988.

Edwin Newman, "Strictly Speaking: Will America be the Death of English?" New York: Warner Books, 1975.

Mary Norris, "Between You & Me: Confessions of a Comma Queen." New York: Norton, 2015.

Joyce Carol Oates, "Soul at the White Heat: Inspiration, Obsession and the Writing Life." New York: Harper Collins, 2016.

Steven Pinker, "The Sense of Style: The Thinking Person's Guide to Writing in the 21st Century." New York: Viking, 2014.

Gabriel L. Rico, "Writing the Natural Way: Using Right-Brain Techniques to Release Your Expressive Powers." Los Angeles: Tarcher, 1983.

Rainer Maria Rilke, "Letters to a Young Poet," revised and reissued edition. New York: W.W. Norton, 2004.

Jordan Rosenfield, "A Writer's Guide to Persistence." Blue Ash, Ohio: Writer's Digest Books, 2015.

Edgar H. Schuster, "Breaking the Rules: Liberating Writers Through Innovative Grammar Instruction." Portsmouth, N.H: Heinemann, 2003.

Helen Sword, "Stylish Academic Writing." Cambridge: Harvard University Press, 2012.

William Strunk, Jr., and E.B. White, "The Elements of Style," 3rd ed. New York: Macmillan, 1979.

Caroline Taggart, "500 Words You Should Know." Buffalo: Firefly Books, 2018.

John R. Trimble, "Writing with Style: Conversations on the Art of Writing," 2nd ed. Englewood Cliffs, N.J.: Prentice Hall, 2000.

Kate L. Turabian, "A Manual for Writers," 9th ed. Chicago: University of Chicago Press, 2007.

David Foster Wallace, "Consider the Lobster, and Other Essays." New York: Back Bay Books, 2007.

Cecelia Watson, "Semicolon: The Past, Present, and Future of a Misunderstood Mark." New York: Ecco, 2019.

Eudora Welty, "One Writer's Beginnings." New York: Warner Books, 1984.

Joseph M. Williams, "Style: Toward Clarity and Grace," rev. ed. Chicago: University of Chicago Press, 2000.

William Zinsser, "On Writing Well," 7th rev. ed. New York: Harper Collins, 2006.

William Zinsser, "Writing with a Word Processor." New York: Harper Trade Books, 1983.

Thanks

I'm indebted to those who have helped edit and suggested improvements on this essay, especially Joe Barrera, Jackson Buckley, Holly Carter, Jim Ciletti, Tania Cronin, Pranit Garg, Michael Genovese, Jon Goldstein, Serena Hoffman, Rebecca Jessup, Robert Knapp, Bob Loevy, David Lowland, Evan Miyawaki, Tom Murawski, Duncan Newcomer, Steven Ortega, Jessica Pauls, Margo Scribner, Carolyn Shultz, John Stith, Rhonda Van Pelt, Devon Weiland and Teddy Weiss.

I thank the American Political Science Association and Prentice-Hall for publishing my earlier essays on this subject. I am grateful to the many students at Princeton, Colorado College and Whitman College who discussed these ideas with me.

Extra-special thanks to Angela Hoy, Ali Hibberts, Todd Engel, Brian Whiddon, Justin Hibberts and the rest of the patient gang at the enterprising Abuzz Press for their guidance in converting my writing into this attractive book.

About the Author

Photo by Devon Weiland.

Tom Cronin is an award-winning political scientist and author of many books including "Imagining a Great Republic," "The State of the Presidency," "Direct Democracy." and "On the Presidency." He is co-author of "Leadership Matters," "The Paradoxes of the American Presidency," "Colorado Politics" and textbooks on American and state politics.

He served as President of Whitman College (1993-2005) and was McHugh Professor of American Institutions and Leadership and an Interim President at Colorado College.

tcronin@coloradocollege.edu

CPSIA information can be obtained
at www.ICGtesting.com
Printed in the USA
BVHW041401120122
625994BV00015B/1702